The Blues Don't Change

By Al Young

Poetry

Dancing (1969)
The Song Turning Back Into Itself (1971)
Geography of the Near Past (1976)

Novels

Snakes (1970)
Who Is Angelina? (1975)
Sitting Pretty (1976)
Ask Me Now (1980)

Anthologies

Yardbird Lives! (with Ishmael Reed, 1978)
Calafía: The California Poetry (with Ishmael Reed, *et al.*, 1979)

Nonfiction

Bodies & Soul: Musical Memoirs (1981)

New and Selected Poems

The Blues Don't Change

by *Al Young*

Louisiana State University Press
Baton Rouge and London   1982

Copyright © 1965, 1966, 1967, 1968, 1969, 1970, 1971, 1972, 1973, 1974, 1975, 1976, 1977, 1978, 1979, 1980, 1981, and 1982 by Al Young
All rights reserved
Manufactured in the United States of America

Design: Patricia Douglas Crowder
Typeface: Garamond #3
Composition: G&S Typesetters, Inc.
Printing and Binding: Thomson Shore, Inc.

LIBRARY OF CONGRESS CATALOGING IN PUBLICATION DATA

Young, Al, 1939–
  The blues don't change.

  I. Title.
PS3575.O683A6 1982   811'.54   81-19356
ISBN 0-8071-0978-9   AACR2
ISBN 0-8071-0979-7

The author would like to thank the editors of the following publications in whose pages many of these poems, some in slightly different form, appeared:
Aftermath of Invisibility (Xavier University), *Aldebaran Review*, *Alpha Sort*, *American Rag*, *Beloit Poetry Journal*, *Black Dialogue*, *Black on Black*, *Brilliant Corners*, *California Poets Anthology* (Second Coming Press), *Camels Coming*, *Chicago Review*, *Confrontation*, *Counter/ Measures*, *Crystalline Flight*, *Decal* (Cardiff, Wales), *Dices* (Houghton Mifflin Co.), *Egg*, *El Corno Emplumado* (Mexico City), *Epoch* (Cornell University), *Essence*, *Evergreen*, *Foothill Quarterly* (Foothill College), *Galley Sail Review*, *Guabi*, *Hambone*, *Hanging Loose*, *Illuminations*, *Iowa Review*, *Jeopardy* (Western Washington University), *Journal for the Protection of All Beings*, *Journal of Black Poetry*, *The Lit*, *Love (Incorporating Hate)*, *Loveletter*, *Loves*, *Etc.* (Doubleday/Anchor), *Massachusetts Review*, *Mosaic: Literature & Ideas* (University of Manitoba Press), *Natural Process* (Hill & Wang), *The New Black Poetry* (International Publishers), *New Directions*, *New Orleans Review* (Loyola University), *New York Review of Books* (*Antaeus* Selection), *Obsidian*, *100 Flowers*, *Paris Review*, *Perspectives*, *Place*, *Quarry* (University of California at Santa Cruz), *Rogue River Gorge*, *San Francisco Bay Guardian*, *San Miguel Review* (Mexico), *Sequoia* (Stanford University), *Sponge*, *23 California Poets*, *Umoja*, *Umbra*, *WPA*, *Wine & Oil Anthology* (Bombay), *Works*, *Yardbird Reader*, and *Y'Bird*; also *The Black Scholar* and *Threepenny Review*.

In memory of my stepbrother
Walter Simmons, Jr.
(1950–1976)

Contents

from Geography of the Near Past (1976)

The Blues Don't Change (New Poems)

Dancing

1969

A Dance for Militant Dilettantes

No one's going to read
or take you seriously,
a hip friend advises,
until you start coming down on them
like the black poet you truly are
& ink in lots of black in your poems
soul is not enough
you need real color
shining out of real skin
nappy snaggly afro hair
baby grow up & dig on *that!*

You got to learn to put in about
stone black fists
coming up against white jaws
& red blood splashing
down those fabled wine & urine-
stained hallways
black bombs blasting out real white estate
the sky itself black with what's to come:
final holocaust
the settling up

Dont nobody want no nice nigger no more
these honkies man that put out
these books & things
they want an angry splib
a furious nigrah
they dont want no bourgeois woogie
they want them a militant nigger
in a fiji haircut
fresh out of some secret boot camp
with a bad book in one hand
& a molotov cocktail in the other
subject to turn up at one of their conferences
or soirees
& shake the shit out of them

A Dance for Li Po

2 lbs bananas
2 rootbeers
4 McIntosh apples
(best of the little ones
which is all that was left)
orange juice
corn
halibut
2 dollars & something
a quick peek inside the bookstore
surrounded by the uppermiddleclass
housewives in expensive boots
hubbies in expensive beards
children got up like film urchins
in funny hats
funny heads

The sky thickens
all the lights come on
I drag it all home
sniffle in the cold
cut across the playground
where kids're chasing after
flies they cant even see
wink at the inevitable moon anyway
have another go at the mailbox

exhale
take my place at the door
come in laughing at the musty corners
dig into the bag
take it all out
stack it all up
sing over the bananas

stand there
just paying visits
to all the good places
Ive been over the years
trying out the different kinds
of darkness

& light
myself but a shadow
on the world wall
unpriced
unbought

gone today
here tomorrow

Dancing Together

Already it's been years
since you surprised me
from the noonday shadows
of my cheap pension
with its empty wine bottles
& sad scrubbed balconies
in a Madrid that long ago
went the way of Moorish ballads
dime romances
upright pianos painted black &
trimmed in lace,
or the red & yellow quivering
of flowers on a hillside
as military aircraft
zooms overhead

Surrounding one another
we swayed in the rickety hallway
laughing at the top of the stairs
like a couple of sweating
hundred dollar gypsies
re-united by an old deep song,

working our helpless magic
one upon the other
word against word
silence against silence,
sorcerers on welfare

Again I wait
& go looking for you
in the shadow of this new night
in which I would bury
the blueness of my thoughts
& my troublesome words
like a musician
after the engagement
packs his instruments away
& encases himself
in the warm dark folds
of a woman's love

A Dance for Ma Rainey

I'm going to be just like you, Ma
Rainey this monday morning
clouds puffing up out of my head
like those balloons
that float above the faces of white people
in the funnypapers

I'm going to hover in the corners
of the world, Ma
& sing from the bottom of hell
up to the tops of high heaven
& send out scratchless waves of yellow

& brown & that basic black honey
misery

I'm going to cry so sweet
& so low
& so dangerous,
Ma,
that the message is going to reach you
back in 1922
where you shimmer
snaggle-toothed
perfumed &
powdered
in your bauble beads

hair pressed & tied back
throbbing with that sick pain
I know
& hide so well
that pain that blues
jives the world with
aching to be heard
that downness
that bottomlessness
first felt by some stolen delta nigger
swamped under with redblooded american agony;
reduced to the sheer shit
of existence
that bred
& battered us all,
Ma,
the beautiful people
our beautiful brave black people
who no longer need to jazz
or sing to themselves in murderous vibrations
or play the veins of their strong tender arms
with needles
to prove that we're still here

Dancing in the Street

for my NYC
summer workshop
students

Just because you wear a natural baby
dont mean you aint got a processed mind.
The field is open
the whole circle of life
is ours for the jumping into,
we ourselves the way we feel
right now
re-creating ourselves
to suit particular dreams & visions
that are no one else's.

Who needs that big mortgaged house
those household finance cars
they advertise
so scientifically
between newscasts,
expensive fronts
those foot-long cigarettes
that brand of breath?

I'd have to travel all the way
back to Lemuria
(cradle of the race
beneath the Pacific)
to bring back a more golden picture of us
the way we looked today
the way we are all the time inside,
healthy black masters
of our own destiny;
set at last on splashing the reins
& shaking off the blinders
that keep the north american
trillion dollar mule team
dragging its collective ass
into that nowhere desert
of bleached white bones & bomb tests.

Dance of the Infidels

in memory of Bud Powell

The smooth smell of Manhattan taxis,
Parisian taxis, it doesnt matter, it's
the feeling that modern man is all youve
laid him out to be in those tinglings & rushes;
the simple touch of your ringed fingers
against a functioning piano.

              The winds of Brooklyn
still mean a lot to me. The way certain chicks
formed themselves & their whole lives around
a few notes, an attitude more than anything.
I know about the being out of touch, bumming
nickels & dimes worth of this & that off
him & her here & there—everything but
hither & yon.

          Genius does not grow on trees.

                            I owe
you a million love dollars & so much more than
thank-you for re-writing the touch & taste & smell
of the world for me those city years when I could
very well have fasted on into oblivion.

                      Ive just
been playing the record you made in Paris with Art
Blakey & Lee Morgan. The european audience
is applauding madly. I think of what Ive heard
of Buttercup's flowering on the Left Bank & days
you had no one to speak to. Wayne Shorter is
beautifying the background of sunlight with
children playing in it & shiny convertibles
& sedans parked along the block as I blow.

                       Grass
grows. Negroes. Women walk. The world, in case
youre losing touch again, keeps wanting the same
old thing.

           You gave me some of it; beauty I sought
before I was even aware how much I needed it.

                                                    I know
this world is terrible & that one must, above all,
hold onto the heart & the hearts of others.

                            I love *you*

Myself When I Am Real

for Charles Mingus

The sun is shining in my backdoor
right now.
                    I picture myself thru jewels
the outer brittleness gone as I
fold within always.   Melting.

Love of life is love of God
sustaining all life,
                            sustaining me
when wrong or un-self-righteous
in drunkenness & in peace.

                            He who loves me
is me. I shall return to Him always,
my heart is rain, my brain earth,
but there is only one sun & forever
it shines forth one endless poem
of which my ranting, my whole life
is but breath.

                    I long to fade back
into this door of sun forever

Dancing

Yes the simplicity of my life
is so complicated,
on & on it goes,
my lady is gone,
she's at work by now
pulling that 4 to midnight shift.
The hours pass,
I make passes at sumptuous shapes
(typewritten you know)
& rediscover that the Muse is a bitch,
any muse,
music
comes into the picture.
I should be out having adventures
like all the other authors
chasing down dialogue
in the fashionable ghettos,
spearing the bizarre,
everything but falling deeper & deeper
into bad habits
into debt
into traps
in to love
in love
in love with strangers.

I couldve been a trench-coated pusher
& dealt heroin to diplomats
or stood around looking innocent enough
& landed up in the dexamil chewinggum nights
with some of the Go-Go girls who really know
Sun Frun Cisco,
like the time you had to lead me around like a sister
& buy me hangover sandwiches;
I went banging into one pay phone after another
& emptied out musta been a good 6 bucks in coins
all toll
& we did a little laughing of our own
on the benches.

But getting by in Never-Never Land is never enough.
Life *is* more than fun & games.
The thought
after all
that either of us is capable of being assassinated
at any moment
for absolutely nothing
& relatively little
is of course unnerving.
The clouds of blue summer
keep getting whiter & thicker
by the afternoon
especially up around the mountains
but nobody cares
in California
nobody dares.

Ladies & gentlemen keep sitting down
at the same old exquisite harpsichords;
bluesmen keep hanging around recording studios
for 3 days in a row
trying to get a hit out of there;
blurry-eyed filipinos
with matching wives or irish girlfriends
keep having a go at pizza
in dim lit parlors run by greeks
served up by lackadaisical she-slavs
from the middlewests,
shy wasps out of Bakersfield.

Kids who werent even born
when I first got on to
how completely the Word can kill
& restore
keep practicing up to tangle with the Man;
drunks & soberer citizens
keep trying to sneak free looks
up inside the topless shoeshine stand
on Columbus Ave,
more post-colonial amuricana;
dogs & cats keep checking out pet food commercials

& running up more in vet bills
than my late grayed grandfather
ever earned,
he was a farmer all right
but who isnt
nowadays
we all keep farming one another
into the ground
& steady losing.
                    Ahhhhhhmerica!
you old happy whore
you miserable trigger-happy cowboy
as bound to death as an overweight film harlot
whose asset's begun to drag
& whose hollywood prophets have to put
the bad mouth out
to gentlemen of the board backeast—
"It's all over dolling
it's *been* all over."
Pity
how fast the deal can go down
when there's nothing
even speculative
to hold it up.

2

In the end there are only beautiful things to say.
Never mind how dirty the floor was
or the mind of the cuban lady across the street
who suspects you of being a filthy drug addict
who heaves stones at his wife every night
& if his house burned down this evening
it wouldnt be any big thing.

There is all this.
There are friends who'll never know
who you really are
& care less;
sick powerful men
in high dizzying places

who do not operate under the influence of music
who would just as soon assassinate
as make a hero of you
once youre no longer capable of
impeding their selfish proposals.
Their children wear sweatshirts
with your face
your hallowed face shines promiscuously
from the fronts of their sweatless children's
T-shirts
& there will be talk of a 6-hour TV spectacular
the combined effort of all the net-
works.
          20th Century Fox is going to do the picture.
The donations come rolling in.

It keeps coming back tho.
Children keep getting themselves born,
the soil that once was sweet to taste
draws up & hardens like cornbread baked too long.
Not a green loving thing emerges.
Our children invade the sea.

Evolving fish
plot revolution
against seething ex-fish
& time is moving it on.

Verily
the power that churns the sea
is a solar delight
a celestial upheaval:
the moon is not the moon we think
but serves.

The moon is your face
in the window of the world
the power heart that pumps beneath
the blood that would splatter every whichway
(as from the bellies of cool slit fish)
coursing to its original destinations
watering insights

bathing our insides
washing the way clear for new origins.

It is inevitable
that we should come to these dark places
to these waters where the drowning
appears to take place &
where attitudes of the ignorant
—our former future selves—
appall us in our journeying forth.
Many's the throat I may have slashed
or angel betrayed
in lives past
out of indignation
thinking it might be one less ass
to contend with
in bringing the promiseland to this planet
here & now
once & for all who counted.

But the knife doubles back
& gets to the point
where environment becomes foul
or the mind has harbored so much pain
that it gives itself up
throws itself away
or collapses
wanting to die
wanting to have been dead
& absent.

3

Be the mystic
& wage ultimate revolution,
be true to your self,
be what you always wanted
but be that.

No need to pack up
rush into hiding
& be teaching hypnotism in Harlem

advanced gun-running in Angola
Lima or Port-au-Prince
or be back on 12th Street
dealing in automatics
before the dramatic eye
of national educational television.

Be the taker by surprise
of CIA-subsidized marimba bands &
disconsolate hindu castaways,
be the avowed lover of
nothing-to-lose niggers
thru whom Ive returned to the scene of our crimes
because of whose endurance
& in whose care
I was first able to discern
the forcefulness of living love
magnetized at last
from its hidingplace:
the lie,
the not-for-real.
Be yourself
man
they always warned.
                Find out
what you really are.
Be that!

4

I have busted my gut enough
in this absurd horserace
where the jockeys are thrown
     from their saddles
and land among the spectators
     Nicanor Parra

Now that some layers have been peeled back
& I can see where dreams I acted out at 15
came true
I want nothing more than

16

the touch of that peace
the digging for which
has rocked me down thru months & years
of nothing doing
getting nowhere
drinking too much in
drowning too little out
desiring to be infinitely drunk
hiding up under the skirts of women
the soft skin
attracting
as it always does
the hard of seeing
the impossible to touch.

Now that I have walked along envying birds
the security of their placement in nature
& on moment's notice
glanced down toward the sea
on a schedule
that doesnt permit me
time to sit much out;
now that some crystallization of what living's about
has taken place
within
I'm content to settle
for nothing less
than the honey itself.
I have tasted the milk &
found it sour.

Heaven was never more delicious
to me: an earth eater
than when rhythmically presented
the April I met a stranger in a street
a mystic
a prophet
a seeker true enough
with no bullshit attached
who looked honestly into my eyes
& explained to me more than where I'd been

or would have to go;
he touched my trembling hand & hinted
what steps I might take to get there.

Now that I have retraced all the old roads
in this road show version of my past
Ive been putting on
for some time
now
I am ready
to fade out of show biz.

Now that I have risen from the long nap
it is again 7:35 pm
of what this morning
was a lucid new day.
Lights are shining from my window.
Outside
new men & women walk toward one another
in a nighttime field of energy.

Warmblooded &
a little confused
I move toward what I'm hoping is the light.

All my struggles have led me to this moment.

May all your struggles lead likewise toward peace.

Let the revolutions proceed!

Dancing Pierrot

The Chinese moon
I knew it once,
I knew the dusty Egypt moon
& the great snow moon of Mexico
back of Mt. Popocatepetl
lifetimes ago
decades
anybody's moment

I know them now
these fat these skinny moons
that offer just so much of themselves
a piece at a time
for just so long

4 moons
3 moons
2 moons
1 moon these moons
the Tokyo moon
Bahia moon
my San Francisco moon
your Tanzanian moon
pouring its light live
into the orifices of women
& men who work thru the night
in order that they might one day
put themselves down
against its illuminated surfaces
armed to the eyes
with star guns

Mad moon
monkey moon
junior moon
crescent moon of Moors
unmapped moon of mind,

sweet dry wine of light
that I drink
with my eyes!

Dancing in the Laundromat
(or, Dust: An Ordinary Song)

I love you
I need you
you in the laundromat
among the telltale result
of the ubiquitous garment industry
shirts & blouses
(we have arms)
bras & the tops of bathingsuits
(you have breasts)
briefs & shorts panties skirts & bottoms
(we have bottoms centers middles stomachs
bellies crotches & cores)
on down to trousers & slacks
& contemporary leg gear butt-
lined whitelined bluelined
roselined blacklined khaki-
lined rainbow clothesline
line up—

I blow you clean low kisses
from transparent lips
of vowel-shaped word
& no-word,
the well sudsed stocking-
feet continuing
the beds & sheets
pillowcases
tender towel & rag
apparel we take for granted,
delight of all but the nakedest eye.

What is it we wear
that never needs washing?

What is it we wear
that never wears?

The Dancer

When white people speak of being uptight
theyre talking about dissolution & deflection
but when black people say uptight
they mean everything's all right.
I'm all right.
The poem brushes gayly past me
on its way toward completion,
things exploding in the background
a new sun
in a new sky
cantaloupes & watermelon for breakfast
in the Flamingo Motel
with cousin Inez
her brown face stretching & tightening
to keep control of the situation,
pretty Indian cheeks
cold black wavelets of hair,
her boyfriend
smiling from his suit.
We discuss concentration camps
& the end of time.
My mustache
wet with cantaloupe juice
would probably singe
faster than the rest of me
like the feathers of a bird over flame
in final solution of
the Amurkan problem.

Ah, Allah,
that thou hast not forsaken me
is proven by the light
playing around the plastic slats
of half-shut venetian blinds
rattling in this room on time
in this hemisphere on fire.
The descendants of slaves
brush their teeth
adorn themselves before mirrors
speak of peace & of living kindness &

touch one another
intuitively & in open understanding.
"It could be the end of the world,"
she says, "they use to didnt be afraid
of us but now that they are
what choice do they have
but to try & kill us?"
but she laughs & I laugh & he laughs
& the calmness in their eyes
reaches me finally
as I dig my spoon into the belly of a melon

The Imitation Dance

Time is Berkeley
the place is now
where some unenlightened children
beyond the rim of my attention
are actively lollygagging
on the hard sidewalk
laid in
where trees once loved so informally,
or dribbling Ishmael Reed's zen basketballs
across the playground in windy spring light.
I make nothing of this until the din subsides
& I'm forced to account for the silence.

Orange juice a roll some lettuce banana/milk
the way we eat now, appearances
real enough
dissolving in the juices

of my hidden stomach.
Form *is* emptiness.
                              Objects clutter my vision:
books beads fern shoes machine-parts a table
a decoration squash a
chance scattering of oolong leaf
the 29¢ teacup & pencils
apple seed a fragrant picture of you
pinned against the wall
to mountains
a TV set that's never worked
some clocks,
a moment,
our plastic cubbyhole in Ha Ha Street.

Everything is supposed to have changed yet
flatulence & decline are still being discussed
with the same open passion
in all but the right places;
I manage to stay as poor as ever,
a part-Indian excavator of old inner cities
out here at the edge of the jungle,
but one day I'm going to move
even further from the so-called center
on into the heart of things.
Years may pass again
or only some hours before I dance out
the shape of another clear day,
eternal unit of forever

April–August 1968

2 Takes from Love in Los Angeles

A potted fern
in a Vine St. apartment
spreads its green delicate tentacles
like my cousin Cynthia
does her fingers
at the piano
in the window
West 27th St
the colored district
where almost everybody
has a REpublic or a 73-
telephone number;
no maps sold
to the homes of these stars:

my Uncle James
game to the end
in his rickety walkup
room on the 2nd floor
with low-rent view
of rooftops & parkinglots
neon liquor messages
where you watch
a dude out of Texas
with a process
& a redhead
turn left
on a red light &
barely miss
getting his jag
smashed to pieces;
Unc is imagining
how many nickel numbers
he'd have to hit
back in Detroit
to get his used car
overhauled again—

James
Cynthia
Richard

Toni
Marti
Inez
Desi
Pierre
their blood my blood
in this other kind of colony

way out west

where the Indians are real
& train for equal opportunity positions,

where the young Chicanos
whip ass
& wig behind
soul music &
Brown is Beautiful,

where lithe &
lipsticked Chinese girls
avoid Japanese advances
maintaining that cool
by any means necessary,

where the keeper of dreams
is solemn &
wears a whole body dickey
from odious head
to fabulous toe
to entice the young women
& other boys

In one dream
the third world ghosts
of Charlie Chan &
Mantan Moreland
in the gentle sting
of a gasoline twilight
take turns
kissing on an unidentified starlet
with a natural &
a bankamericard

Even the flourishing nazi
whose children smoke opium
& inject themselves
for laughs in Orange County
has his angeleno mistresses,
intelligent negresses
in auburn wig
& shades;
strange thin-lipped aryans
whose underwear glitters,
new Marilyn Monroes
in colorfast fashion knits
parking their cars
in puddles of quicksilver
who wink at spooks
propped next to palmtrees

Love licks its lip
at no one

A Dance for Aging Hipsters

For the aging hipster
there isnt any cure,
as he fumbles the key
to his own front door
it gives & opens anyway

Loaded again yes
it's him & he's loaded again
this time on time but
the very mellowness he fathered
& nurtured thru high spring

has fallen now
into an earlier autumn
than even he
had anticipated

Dreamily he clings
to his favorite memories
of splendid explosions
that titillated the glands,
cold implosions
in the blue of his heart
& he suffers leftover visions
of festive backrooms
on crazy warm nights
where he jived other jivers
& set the pace
for a whole nervous subculture
strung out behind loneliness

Dancing All Alone

We move thru rooms & down the middle of freeways,
myself & I.
A feeling lumps up in the throat
that says I wont be living forever.
The middle of the month signifies
the end of some beginning
the beginning of some end.
Once I thought the heart could be ripped out
like doll filling
& naked essence examined
but I'm a man

not a mannikin.
I would transfer to the world
my idea of what it's like beneath flesh & fur.
I cannot do this without making fools of myself.
Cold winds whoosh down on me under winter stars
& the way ahead is long but not uncertain.
I am neither prince nor citizen
but I do know what is noble in me
& what is usefully vulgar.
It is from this point that the real radiates.
I move & am moved,
do & am done for.
My prison is the room of myself
& my rejection of both is my salvation,
the way out being the way in,
the freeway that expands to my true touch,
a laughter in the blood that dances.

Dear Arl

Sweets you were glittering this morning
brushing your teeth with no more Crest
& me lying there need to get up
grouching in the form of my self stupid

You just said what you had to say
& let me go my way complaining about
shirts & cooking which I dont really care about
hardly even think about really except
to happy music in the afternoon awake

Well I got the money & bought some books
& had a cheeseburger & dish of beans at Kip's

with Tom Glass who put me in a good mood
talking about people making comebacks—
"What a sad scene a cat who has to think
                in those terms even
as if to say I'm in style now folks but
                watch out
I'm subject to fade out any minute now"

I'd change her sad rags into glad rags
                if I could
sing The Four Seasons on KYA radio twelve sixty
                San Fran Cisco—
Youre taking the F bus to the city tonight
straight from work to buy another pretty
for your wardrobe still growing 2 dresses now
& I have to be in show biz at The Jabberwock
for $17.50 which is current union scale
                Wow!

Redbeans & rice on stove & squash coming up,
no idea whether youll like the dinner—

I think of you alone picking over nylons
& slips & sweet little sweaters on sale,
moving up Grant Ave with that special switch
which isnt really a switch at all but your self
                walking
I like your walk & taste & your dresses,
also the way you counter my crabbiness,
                yes—
then too I love you & all the rest of it

Lemons, Lemons

Hanging from fresh trees
or yellow against green
in a soft blaze of afternoon
while I eat dutifully
my cheese & apple lunch
or the coolness of twilight
in some of these California towns
I inhabited a lifetime ago.

Hung that way
filled up with sunlight
like myself ripe with light
brown with light & ripe with shadow
the apple red & gold & green with it
cheese from the insides of
sun-loving cows

Sweet goldenness of light
& life itself
sunny at the core
lasting all day long
into night
into sleep
permeating dream shapes
forming tingly little words
my 2¢ squeezed out
photosynthetically
in hasty praise
of lemon/light

Paris

I couldnt ever tell you
just what might have been going on,
the gray brick nowhereness
of certain gendarmes
if you can dig it

But for now
you follow me into ice cream places
where they push hamburgers
& beer too
where nothing seems to have changed
since Worcester,
where I can feel the flirtiness
of meat heat rising in the streets,
a european princess
easing herself up next to me
dead on the Champs Elysées

I buy my *jetons*
& make phonecalls like a nice fellow
to whom directions are mapped out sweetly
by tender old ladies born in Rue La Bruyere
as all the african brothers
hop on & off the metro
jammed up with birds & algerians

England no
this is France
another colonial power environment
far from Richard Wright's
or my own wrong Mississippi

Encircled by luminous space
I lay my woolly head
against your tan belly of Italy
& listen to the fat cars in the streets
hometown of the bourgeoisie
& clean creamy ladies & you
sparkle darkly
where I too
am pregnant
with astonishment

Reading Nijinsky's Diary

for JoAnne

Who of us is not mad

I am set loose again
Moved beyond tears
by perfect utterance
—cut loose, freed
to know ever for all
as I did so perfectly
long ago & all ways
that poem story book
all play on nothing
if not skin
to house truths
spurting up no where

I have been ragged
hair uncombable
licking sour lips
mounting floor heat
that it may rise
up my slept-in limbs

Morning explodes
behind my eyes,
I dance out into a rain
forest of bodily concern,
vine-tangled nerve
crash & trip into
sweet leaf trees
to teach me roots
& branches of becoming

Becoming receptor of
Life Death & Feeling
you need only speak,
"My madness is my love
for mankind," for me
to be sane again

Birthday Poem

First light of day in Mississippi
son of laborer & of house wife
it says so on the official photostat
not son of fisherman & child fugitive
from cottonfields & potato patches
from sugarcane chickens & well-water
from kerosene lamps & watermelons
mules named jack or jenny & wagonwheels,

years of meaningless farm work
work Work WORK WORK WORK—
"Papa pull you outta school bout March
to stay on the place & work the crop"
—her own earliest knowledge
of human hopelessness & waste

She carried me around nine months
inside her fifteen year old self
before here I sit numbering it all

How I got from then to now
is the mystery that could fill a whole library
much less an arbitrary stanza

But of course you already know about that
from your own random suffering
& sudden inexplicable bliss

A Little More Traveling Music

A country kid in Mississippi I drew water
        from the well
& watched our sun set itself down behind
        the thickets,

hurried from galvanized baths to hear music
over the radio—Colored music, rhythmic & electrifying,
more Black in fact than politics & flit guns.

Mama had a knack for snapping juicy fruit gum
& for keeping track of the generation of chilrens
she had raised, reared & no doubt forwarded,
rising thankfully every half past daybreak
to administer duties the poor must look after
if theyre to see their way another day, to eat, to live.

I lived & upnorth in cities sweltered & froze,
          got jammed up & trafficked
in everybody's sun going down but took up with the
          moon
as I lit about getting it all down up there
where couldnt nobody knock it out.

Picking up slowly on the gists of melodies, most noises
          softened.
I went on to school & to college too, woke up cold
& went my way finally, classless, reading all poems,
          some books & listening to heartbeats.

Well on my way to committing to memory the ABC
          reality,
I still couldnt forget all that motherly music,
those unwatered songs of my babe-in-the-wood days
until, committed to the power of the human voice,
I turned to poetry & to singing by choice,
reading everyone always & listening, listening for a
          silence deep enough
to make out the sound of my own background music.

1962–1967

Dancing Day to Day

In my street
the people mostly go.
Very few come
to what I'd call home.

We earn our wages
cash our checks
park our cars
manage our packages
receive our mail
whistle our tunes
sweep our porches
& draw our curtains
in public.

My neighbors are
black
mexican
japanese
chinese
even a young couple from India
& straight-out ordinary gringos
(one of whom
strolls her senile bull terrier
around the block
twilights
with a baseball bat).

They dont go climbing
the lemontree
or shaking the appletree
out back for fun.
They mow their lawns
smoke their grass
crank up the stereo
or the TV volume
evenings
or wash dolls
& set them out to dry.

One of my favorites
is the little boy

whose new bike gets a flat
or who mopes across the schoolyard
kicking stones
like little footballs.

Best of all
since moving here
I like going for walks
or for drowsy car rides
with the glamorous woman
in the stylish clothes
who loves newspapers
magazines
& lives in number 2.

When she knocks at my door
frustrated
after hours
& falls into me
bearing aromatic kisses
it relaxes me
nights
when I'm afraid
the loud dizzy lady upstairs
is finally going to topple
down thru the ceiling
or at least snap
& pitch the fit
we've all felt coming

The Song Turning Back Into Itself

1971

Loneliness

The poet is the dreamer.
He dreams that the clock stops
& 100 angels wandering wild
drift into his chamber
where nothing has been settled

Should he get himself photographed
seated next to a mountain
like Chairman Mao
the real sun flashing golden
off his real eyes
like the light off stones
by oceans?

Give me your perfect hand
& touch me simply with a word,
one distillation of forever

Should he put his white tie on
with his black shirt
& pass himself off as a docile gangster
for the very last time?

The poet's dream is real
down to the last silver bullet
Should he slip again to Funland
in the city & throw dimes down holes
to watch hungry women flicker
one hair at a time
in kodacolor
from sad civilized boxes?

Should he practice magic
on politicians &
cause them to crack their necks
in a laughing fit?

The poet is the dreamer.
He dreams babies asleep in wombs
& counts the wasted sighs
lost in a flake of dusty semen
on a living thigh
Should he dream the end of an order

the abolition of the slave trade,
the restoration to life
of dead millions
filing daily past time clocks
dutifully gorging themselves
on self-hatred & emptiness?

Should he even dream
an end to loneliness,
the illusion that
we can do without
& have no need
of one another?

It is true that he needs you,
I need you,
I need your pain & magic,
I need you now more than ever
in every form & attitude—
gesturing with a rifle in your hand
starving in some earthly sector
or poised in heavenly meditation
listening to the wind
with the third ear
or staring into forever
with the ever-watchful third eye,
you are needed

The poet is the dreamer &
the poet is himself the dream
& in this dream
he shares your presence

Should he smash down walls
& expose the ignorance
beneath our lying noisiness?

No! No!
the gunshot he fires
up into the silent air
is to awaken

Friday the 12th

Floating thru morning
    I arrive at afternoon
& see the bright lightness
    light ness
    of it all

& thank God
& go on living
taking spoiled strawberries
& a tapioca pudding gone bad
    out the ice box

Must wash my hair &
    go get it cut off my head
    head itches
Notice my luck changes
    when I've had
    a hair cut
same as if I dont rise before noon
    the day doesnt go right

Afternoon becomes evening becomes night

There're worlds into worlds between all worlds
    so dont worry
    about divisions of day
for even when I fall asleep the day
    wont have ended
    wont have begun

In fact years whoosh by in time for me
    to see myself as endless fool child
& to learn better than
    to laugh at such conditions

Now I bathe & go out into the streets
    airplane raging overhead
    (your head perhaps)
    reminding me how
    even floating must come to an end

Erosong

I first saw you in a trance
(you were in the trance, not me).
Me I was dancing

on turbulent waters.
All my shores had been pulled up
& naked I was nowhere

but there was some drowsy grace you offered,
some rendezvous from way-back to be fulfilled.
I moved toward you

saying everything,
you nothing.
The 20th century moon

did its turn-around,
revealing how much the sun it was
in the face of your light,

all that light,
in the daytime,
at night

The Old Fashioned Cincinnati Blues

for Jesse "Lone Cat" Fuller

O boy the blues!
I sure do love blues
but the blues dont like me

This is Cincinnata Ohia 1949
& that's me & my brother Frank
in the NY Central Train Station

trying to get it together
on our way down
to Meridian Mississippi
where later I hid
in cornfields, smoked butts &
dreamed all about
the sunny grownup future,
dreamed about Now

Ah but that Now that
Right Now that is,
all I wanna dream about's
that NY Cincy Terminal
that summer with its intervals
of RC Cola Coolers,
tin tub baths taken
one at a time
back behind the evening stove—

Chickens—

Our grandmother
(Mrs. Lillian Campbell)

Cousin George & Uncle John
swapping ghost stories
Saturday nite—

O Americana!
United Statesiana!

A lonesome high,
a funnytime cry,
the blues
the blues
the blues

The Problem of Identity

Used to identify with my father first making me want to be a gas station
    attendant simple drink coca-cola listen to the radio, work on people's cars,
    hold long conversations in the night black that clean gas smell of oil &
    no-gas, machine coolness, rubber, calendars, metal sky, concrete, the
    bearing of tools, the wind—true Blue labor Red & White

Identified with Joe Louis: Brown Bomber, you know They'd pass along the
    mud streets of Laurel Mississippi in loudspeaker truck, the white folks,
    down by where the colored schools was & all of us, out there for Recess or
    afterschool are beckoned to come get your free picture of Joe Louis,
    C'mon & get it kids it's Free, c'mon naow—What it is is Chesterfield
    cigarettes in one corner of the beautiful slick photo of Mr. Louis is the
    blurb, *Joe like to smoke too, see, and he want all yall to follow right long
    in his footsteps & buy up these here chesterfields & smoke your little hoodies
    off & youll be able to step up in that ring begloved & punch a sucker out.*
    It was the glossiness of the photo, I finally figured out years later, that
    had me going—didnt really matter whose picture was on it altho it was
    nice to've been Joe's because he was about as great as you could get
    downsouth, post world war II as the books say

Identified with Otis (think his name was) worked at grocery store in Ocean
    Springs, came by, would sit & draw on pieces of brown paperbag, drew
    in 1940s style of cartoons bordering on "serious" sketching, i.e., in the
    manner of those sultan cartoons with the harem gals by that black
    cartoonist Sims you see em all the time in old *Esquires* & *Playboys*. Well,
    that's the way Otis could draw & he'd show me in the make-do
    livingroom seated on do-fold how to do a portrait of a chic perfect anglo-
    featured woman, say, in profile out of his head built mostly from
    magazine & picture-show impressions, & he could draw lots of world
    things, drew me for instance

Later Otis went up to Chicago, sadness, madness, wed, bled, dope, hopeless,
catapulted into the 20th century like the rest of us—rudely,

                                  steeped in
homemade makeshift chemical bliss of/or flesh, waiting for nothing less than
The Real Thing

Pachuta, Mississippi / A Memoir

                    I too
                once lived
            in the country

                        Incandescent
                            fruits
                        in moonlight
                    whispered to me
                        from trees
                            of
                1950
                swishing
                    in the green nights

                                wavelengths away
                                        from
                                tongue-red meat
                                    of melon

                            wounded squash
                        yellow as old afternoons

                                chicken
                                    in love
                                        with calico

                            hiss & click of flit gun

                        juice music
                            you suck up
                        lean stalks of field cane

                                        Cool as sundown
                                        I lived there too

For JoAnne in Poland

You are not to trouble yourself
with your ladyness
your blackness,
mysteries
of having been brought up
on collard greens
                bagels
                        &
                        Chef-Boy-Ar-Dee

Nor must you let the great haters
of our time
rattle in your heart

They are small potatoes
whose old cries
for blood
may be heard
any afternoon of the millennium
any portion
            of this
                    schoolroom globe

Old Light

How quickly morphology
        shifts
                the whole landscape
        thrice uprooted
                all the tall redwoods
        yanked & shipped to Japan
                since you snapped
                        that one

46

My eyes grow new
         the smile crookeder—
                  Here your coloring
     shines out of you differently
              as tho measured thru
     some other kind of prism
                  one by which the wavelength
                           of a smile
                  is easily recorded

Like distant hills by moonlight
         your own dark beauty
                  brightens
     like meanings of remembered places
              illuminated
                       by time & distance

                  Carmel Valley
                  the Zoo at the end
                           of the Judah line
                  Tomales Bay
                  McGee Street
                  Smith Grade Road
                  Avenida Cinco de Mayo
                  Guadalajara Guadalajara
                  the beach at Point Reyes of
                           saying goodbye
                  to sand the ocean the untakeable
                      sea breeze
                                    doorway
                                       backyard
                                       garden
                                    alleyway
                                       bench
                                    forest of countryside & city

         The passing of time will
                  shatter your heart
                           recorded in
                  mute shadow & light
                           the photographer's hour

The Song Turning Back Into Itself 1

I sing folk tunes unrhymed.
With my heart keeping the beat,
Trust your sorrow, then, to my bosom
Where it will find its cure.
    Li Chin-fa

Breathing in morning
breezing thru rainbows
vanishing in my own breath mist,
how can I still not feel
this warm beat of beats
my own heart of hearts,

myself: an articulate colored boy
who died lucky
who wouldve kept talking himself
into dying,
creatively of course,
the soulful touch
pulsing thru his nervous system
like light thru the arteries of trees,

that mystified young man
whose stupidity knew no bounds
& at whose touch
gold shriveled to tinfoil
wine gurgled into faucet water,

a firstclass fuckup
who but for divine mercy
would have gone
out of commission
long ago
would have become
the original loveboat
cracked up against rocks
in fog or funk,
the rocks in his hard nappy head

the fog in his big blind eyes
the funk in his & everyone's blood
held in
waiting,

waiting

The Song Turning Back Into Itself 2

A song for little children

Always it's either
a beginning
or some end:
the baby's being born
or its parents are
dying, fading on
like the rose
of the poem
withers, its light going out
while gardens come in
to bloom

Let us stand on streetcorners
in the desolate era
& propose a new kind
of craziness

Let us salute one another
one by one
two by two
the soft belly
moving toward
the long sideburns
the adams apple
or no apple at all

Let there be
in this craziness
a moon
a violin
a drum

Let the beautiful brown girl
join hands with
her black sister
her golden sister
her milkskinned sister
their eternal wombs
turning with the moon
Let there be a flute

to squeal above
the beat & the bowing
to open us up
that the greens
the blues
the yellows
the reds
the silvers &
indescribable rusts
might flow out
amazingly
& blend
with the wind

Let the wobbly spin
of the earth
be a delight
wherein
a caress forms
the most perfect circle

Let the always be love
the beginning be love
love the only
possible
end

The Song Turning Back Into Itself 3

Ocean Springs Missippy
you dont know about that
unless youve died in magnolia
tripped across the Gulf
& come alive again
or fallen in the ocean
lapping up light
like the sun digging
into the scruffy palm leaves
fanning the almighty trains
huffing it choo-choo
straight up our street
morning noon & nighttrain
squalling that moan
like a big ass blues man
smoking up the sunset

Consider the little house
of sunken wood
in the dusty street
where my father would
cut his fingers
up to his ankles
in fragrant coils
of lumber shavings
the backyard of nowhere

Consider Nazis & crackers
on the same stage
splitting the bill

Affix it all to
my memory of Ma
& her love of bananas
the light flashing
in & out of our lives
lived 25¢ at a time
when pecans were in season
or the crab & shrimp
was plentiful enough
for the fishermen

to give away for gumbo
for a soft hullo
if you as a woman
had the sun in your voice
the wind over your shoulder
blowing the right way
at just that moment in history

The Song Turning Back Into Itself 4

I violinize peace
in the Nazi era;
semen-colored doves
perched atop sea trains
from the decks of which
women are singing
anti-death songs;
magnificent birds
flap in & out
of tonal pictures
before disappearing
into the green
the blue
the rolling white
of an oceanic music

Tipping thru this skylight
along rooftops
to snuggle in
quaintly
with paintable pigeons
I can still feel
the red & white
the blood sonata
cello'd from me
bow against bone
finger pluck of flesh
as
    I
       laugh
                colors
into your warm wet mouth

Behold dogcatchers
the lady watchers
the simple twist of hip
as it cuts electric air
bringing endless delight
I would walk you up trees
& inscribe at the tops

in leaves
these very words
Let us change the design
of their celluloid architecture
into a shape where love could live
(in street Spanish & Swahili)

This music is real

Feel the rhythm

the lips

Feel today

vibrating

in the throat

Feel sound

Feel space

O feel the presence of

light

brighter than distant circuses

in the child night

of the soul

The Prestidigitator 1

What you gonna do when they burn your barrelhouse down?
What you gonna do when they burn your barrelhouse down?
Gonna move out the piano & barrelhouse on the ground.
    Traditional Afro-American blues

A prestidigitator makes things disappear,
vanish, not unlike a well-paid bookkeeper
or tax consultant or champion consumer

The poet is a prestidigitator, he makes
your old skins disappear & re-clothes you
in sturdy raiment of thought, feeling, soul,

dream & happenstance. Consider him villain of
the earthbound, a two-fisted cowboy with
pencil in one hand & eraser in the other

dotting the horizon of your heart with cool
imaginary trees but rubbing out more than he
leaves in for space so light can get thru.

The Prestidigitator 2

I draw hats on rabbits, sew women back
together, let fly from my pockets flocks of
vibratory hummingbirds. The things Ive got

up my sleeve would activate the most listless
of landscapes (the cracked-earth heart of a bigot,
say) with pigeons that boogaloo, with flags that

light up stabbed into the brain. Most of all it's
enslaving mumbo-jumbo that I'd wipe away, a trick
done by walking thru mirrors to the other side

The Curative Powers of Silence

Suddenly
I touch upon wordlessness,
I who watch Cheryl
the blind girl who lives up the street
walking at night
when she thinks no one's looking
deliberately heading into hedges & trees
in order to hug them
& to be kissed,
thus are we each
hugged & kissed.

Wordless
I fill up
listening for nothing
for nothing at all

as when in so-called life
I am set shivering with warmth
by a vision
with the eyes closed
of the Cheryl in me
when I think no one's looking,
plopped down in a field of grass
under watchful trees
letting the pre-mind dream
of nothing at all
nothing at all
no flicker
no shadow
no voice
no cry,

not even dreaming

—being dreamed

Sunday Illumination

Ive found peace & it's good sleeping late today—head full of eternal ideas,
eternal emptiness; Phil Elwood jazz on KPFA, my wife sunny in tattered
red skirt & sea blue T shirt on back yard grass getting her Spanish lesson

"How would I say: Friday I went to a party & heard some good gospel
music?"—& I try to explain the preterit & the imperfect perfectly
WHEW! but keep interrupting her with poems & to watch a young bee
zero in on flaming fuchsia branches, wondering if flower & insect survive
ex-lives

Then we go hiking in the Berkeley hills first time all year since Europe,
marriage, satori in the slums—New houses have sprung up, split-level
clutter; a half finished trap is going up on the spot top of Dwight Way
where we'd sit on a pile of lumber for panoramic vista of Berkeley
Oakland Alcatraz in the Bay & dazzling San Francisco in the sun—What
was it like here before the invasions?

So by now I got to pee & head aches from heat & climb & hot dogs we bought
& ate walking for breakfast, foul fare—no place to sit—Some affluent
dogs in heat trail us round a bend—the old motorcycle trail looks
dangerously uninteresting, guys go up there scrambling & fall—My
shirt's sticking to my sweat & the friends we thought we'd drop in on,
whatve we to say to them after all?

Descending Arden Steps I make water on a bush, she covering for me—
humorous taboo—then comes our pause on the stone bench where we
almost ruled out wedlock that torturous fall twilight of long ago
Campanile carillon woe

Time to count our blessings as in my heart all pain ceases & for the longest
moment all day I see my sad funny self on earth & the gentle terror of her
female soul, beautiful, but we're alive NOW accumulating karma, no
time to hide in places—no place to hide in time.

Dream Take: 22

Some old Mexico Lisbon set
rainy at night & shimmery.
I alone flop around in midnight,
see everything from angel angle.

New moonless couples mourn by
arm in arm & all hands
after evenings of being quiet,
for soon whatever's to happen's

happened already, always has.
I smile out over the situation
to keep their tears to myself,
tired of time & so much in need of

this mirage of lovers parading.
Safe, I can sense that I'm soon to
awake with no possible camera
to record what I just saw asleep

April Blue

It's time the clock got thrown out the window
& the difference between waking & sleeping
be left undeclared, unassumed.
                              It's the
heart's turn to do a few spins in its fluid.

It's time the birds that play in the street
(that you had to slow down for this morning)
flew to your machine & introduced themselves.

It's time you silenced the radio, the stereo,
the TV, the tea kettle, the kettle drum &

flew to where the inner ear beckons, where
closed eyes have always tingled to take you,
to the end of space if necessary, to the place
the horizon's always promised, to a glowing
spirit world where you'd as soon eat as not,
as soon drink as not, as soon make love as not,
as soon be water as air, as soon be moon as sun.

It's time you made yourself beautiful again,
spreading like color in every direction,
rising & rising to every occasion.
        Summer
may be coming in, maybe not, this painful year.

Spring is the thing that your window frames now.

It's time you soaked in the new light & laughed.

Groupie

Evening isnt so much a playland as it is
a rumpus room, a place where harmony
isnt always complementary & where
spaces between palmtrees of the heart
arent always so spread out.
       By 3 A.M.
there's love in her hose for the sailor
of saxophones or guitars & she'll try & take
the whole night into her skilled mouth
as tho that were the lover she really wanted
to rub against when all the time true love
inhabits her own fingernails & unshaven body.

You love her for the mental whore she is,
the clothed sun in Libra, the horny sister
who with her loose hair flying can get
no better attention for the time being

One West Coast

for Gordon Lapides

Green is the color of everything
that isnt brown, the tones ranging
like mountains, the colors changing.

You look up toward the hills & fog—
the familiarity of it after so many years
        a resident tourist.

                        A young man walks
toward you in vague streetcrossing denims
& pronounced boots. From the pallor of
        his gait, the orange splotch twin gobs of sunset
        in his shades, from the way he vibrates
        his surrounding air, you can tell, you can tell
                he's friendly, circulating,

                        he's a Californian: comes to visit,
                        stays for years, marries, moves a wife in,
                kids, wears out TV sets, gets stranded on
                                loneliness,
                        afternoon pharmaceutica,
                so that the sky's got moon in it by
                        3 o'clock, is blooo, is blown—

The girls: theyre all
winners reared by grandmothers & CBS.

Luckier ones get in a few dances with
mom, a few hours, before dad goes back
in the slam, before "G'bye I'm off
to be a singer!" & another runaway
Miss American future drifts
over the mountain &
into the clouds.

Still
there's a beautifulness about California.
It's based on the way each eyeblink toward
the palms & into the orange grove leads backstage
into the onionfields.

Unreachable, winter happens inside you.

Your unshaded eyes dilate at the spectacle.

You take trips to contain the mystery.

Lonesome in the Country

How much of me is sandwiches radio beer?
How much pizza traffic & neon messages?
I take thoughtful journeys to supermarkets,
philosophize about the newest good movie,
camp out at magazine racks & on floors,
catch humanity leering back in laundromats,
invent shortcuts by the quarter hour.

There's meaning to all this itemization
& I'd do well to look for it in woodpiles

& in hills & springs & trees in the woods
instead of staying in my shack all the time
thinking too much,
                    falling asleep in old chairs

All those childhood years spent in farmhouses
& I still cant tell one bush from another—
Straight wilderness would wipe me out
faster than cancer from smoking cigarettes

My country friends are out all day long
stomping thru the woods all big-eyed &
that's me walking the road afternoons,
head in some book,
                    all that hilly sweetness wasting

Late January
Sonoma Mountain Road
in the Year of the Dragon

Topsy: Part 2

How overwhelming
that Lester tune
heard just out of the rain
early one night
in a cafe bar
full of African students
midtown Madrid
September 1963
young & dumb & lonesome
a long ways from home

amazed at my tall
cheap rum & coke
patting the wetness
from my leathered foot
to that Lester tune
cut by Cozy Cole
blown from a jukebox
right up the street from where
Quixote's Cervantes once died

I Arrive in Madrid

The wretched of the earth
are my brothers.
Neither priest
nor state
nor state of mind
is all God is
who must understand
to have put up for so long
with my drinking & all my restlessness
my hot & cold running around
unwired
to any dogma;
the way I let the eyes
of dark women
in southern countries
rock my head
like a translucent vessel
in turbulent waters.

Long have I longed for adventure,
a peculiar kind of romance
on the high seas of this planet.
Victimized at last
I float alone
exploring time
in search of tenderness,
a love
with no passage attached.

So this is dictatorship,
a watery monday morning
smell of the atlantic
still blowing thru me.
If you have ever died or been born
you will understand
when I speak of everything being salty
like the taste of my mother's tears
when I came back to earth
thru her
after much of the bombing & blood-letting
had taken place here
when Spain was the name of some country
she knew from the words of some popular song
publicized over the radio.

This city too
feels as tho it's held together by publicity
but publicity is going to lose its power
over the lives of men
once we have figured out just what within us
is more powerful & more beautiful than program or text.

For now
there is language & Spanish to cope with,
there are eyelashes & chromosomes
pesetas pounds francs & dollars
& a poverty even wine cannot shut out.

Malagueña Salerosa

for Roberto Mates & for Doris

What beautiful eyes youve got there
underneath your own two eyebrows
underneath your own two eyebrows
what beautiful eyes youve got there

That's Mexican for O youre too much!
I always loved that mariachi song,
learned it on the Three Gold Star Bus
runs out of ratty Tijuana on out
thru dusty Sonora where they stop you
for no reason to search your bags
as if to ask that you promise you wont
do poems about simply what happens,
on up to Michoacán my green Indian dream
to the top of it all—Mexico D.F.

There one night in the big city
Bob & I were happy & fantastic
tripping up Calle Shakespeare,
bourgeois part of town with maids,
arm in arm with joyous Doris
stuck on her NYC politician lover,
Bob brooding his Havana heaven,
me so sad for my only California

We molest a *macho* a jitterbug—
"How far's it from here to Yucatán?"
"Ay hombre as far as I am dronk!"
—only so much kinder in Spanish spoken

Then the four of us arms all linked
danced all the way to quiet Michelet
to serenade young Lady D. goodnight

This Mexico City's vanished.
Bob's back in Detroit working welfare.
Doris whoever she was is no more.
There's isn't any such jitterbug drunk.
The me of then is gone forever

Good thing the song's still around

Moon Watching by Lake Chapala

I love to cross a river in very
bright moonlight and see the
trampled water fly up in chips
of crystal under the oxen's feet.
          The Pillow Book of Sei Shōnagon,
                    10th Century

IT CAN BE beautiful this sitting by oneself all alone except for the world, the
very world a literal extension of living leaf, surface & wave of light: the moon
for example. American poet Hazel Hall felt,
          "I am less myself
          & more of the sun"
                              which I think upon these cool common
nights being at some remove, in spirit at least, from where they are busy
building bombs & preparing concentration camps to put my people into; I am
still free to be in love with dust & limbs (vegetable & human) & with lights in
the skies of high spring.

IN THE AFTERNOON you watch fishermen & fisherboys in mended boats
dragging their dark nets thru the waters. You can even buy a little packet of
dried sardines like I do, a soda, & lean against the rock & iron railings but you
wont be able to imagine the wanderings of my own mustachio'd dad who was a
fisherman in Mississippi in the warm streams of the Gulf of Mexico. I low time
loops & loops! Already I'm drunk with the thought of distances. I do that look
skyward & re-chart the constellations. No one to drop in on. No one to drop in
on me. It's been a long time since I've had nothing better to do than establish
myself in one spot & stare directly into the faces of the moon, the golden
orange white brown blue moon, & listen to the tock of my heart slowing down
in the silence. I can almost hear in the breeze & picture in the sniffable award-
winning moonlight the doings & dyings of my hard-working father, of all my
heartbroken mamas & dads.

WHO WILL LIVE to write The Role of Moonlight in the Evolution of
Consciousness?

IN NEW YORK, San Francisco & points in between the sad young men &
women are packaging their wounds & hawking them; braggadocios cleansing
old blood from syringes & sly needles in preparation for fresh offerings of cold
hard chemical bliss: ofays wasted on suburban plenitude; not-together Bloods
strung out on dreams.

I'M OUT HERE alone, off to one side, in the soft dark inspecting a stripe of tree shadow on my moonlit hand, dissolving into mineral light, quivering donkey light, the waters churning with fish & flora, happiness circulating thru my nervous system like island galaxies thru space.

MEXICO CAN BE Moon can be Madness can be Maya. But the rising notion that we are in the process of evolving from ape to angel under the influence of star-gazing is the Dream.

Detroit 1958

Only parts of the pain of living
may be captured in a poem or
tale or song or in the image seen.

Even in life we only halfway feel
the tears of a brother or sister,
mass disenchantment in cities,
our discovery of love's meagerness,
the slow rise and fall of the sun.

Sadness is the theme of existence;
joy its variations. Pain is only a portion
of sadness, and efforts to escape it
can lead to self-destruction,
one aspect of pain lived imaginatively.

It is in life that we celebrate pain;
It is an art that we imitate it.

Beauty is saddening, or, as the man sings,
"The bitter note makes the song so sweet."

Squirrels

Squirrels are skittering
outside thru the trees
of my bedroom window,
laying it on the line
of my consciousness

Brown & black, furry &
scurrying, how can I not
help loving them like
an old bopster loves licks
laid down building up
so many beats to the moment?

Squirrels may be crazy
but they arent dullards
They like to play too
They cant be hustling nuts &
hoard all the time. Like
everybody else they love
a good chase now & again

Swishing thru branch leaves,
drumming on my diamond roof,
the shining young squirrels
are making & saving the day

Tribute

Yes brothers you invented jazz
& now I'm inventing myself
as lean & prone to deviance
as the brilliance of your
musical utterance, a wind

that sweeps again & again
thru my American window

What a life you sent me
running out into expecting
everyone to know at once
just what it was I was
talking or not talking about

The genius of our race
has far from run its course
& if the rhythms & melody
I lay down this long street
to paradise arent concrete
enough it can only be because
lately Ive grown used to taking
a cozier route than that of
my contemporary ancestors

Where you once walked or ran
or railroaded your way thru
I now fly, caressing the sturdy
air with balls of my feet
flapping my arms & zeroing

The Move Continuing

All beginnings start right here.
The sun & moons of our spirit
keep touching.
I look out the window at rain
& listen casually to latest developments
of the apocalypse
over the radio
barely unpacked &
hear you shuttling in the backgrounds
from one end of the new apartment
to the other
bumping into boxes of personal belongings
I cant remember having touched 48 hours ago.
Jazz
a very ancient music
whirls beneficently
into our rented front room.

I grow back thru years
to come upon myself
shivering
in my own presence of long ago
when the bittersweet world
passed before
(rather than thru)
me
a vibrant collage
of delights
in supercolor.

It wasnt difficult becoming a gypsy.
At one end of the line
there was God.
& at the very other end
there is God.
In between
shine all the stars of all the spaces
illuminating everything
from the two tender points
that are your eyes
to the musical instruments

of these strong but gentle black men
glowing on the LP in the dark,
the darkness of my own heart
beating its way along
thru all the evenings
that lengthen my skies,
all the stockings
that have ever been rolled down
sadly,
lover & beloved
reaching
to touch one another
at this different time
in this different place
as tho tonight were only the beginning
of all those
yester-
days

For Poets

Stay beautiful
but dont stay down underground too long
Dont turn into a mole
or a worm
or a root
or a stone

Come on out into the sunlight
Breathe in trees
Knock out mountains
Commune with snakes
& be the very hero of birds

Dont forget to poke your head up
& blink
Think
Walk all around
Swim upstream

Dont forget to fly

Geography of the Near Past

1976

For Arl in Her Sixth Month

Cool beneath melon-colored cloth, your belly—
a joyous ripening that happens & happens,
that gently takes root & takes over,
a miracle uncelebrated under an autumn dress
that curves & falls slowly to your ankles.

As you busy yourself with backyard gardening,
humming, contained, I think of your tongue
at peace in its place; another kind of fruit,
mysterious flower behind two lips that open
for air & for exits & entrances.

                    Perhaps if I placed
my hungry ear up next to a cantaloupe or coconut
(for hours at a time & often enough),
I'd hear a fluttering or maybe a music almost like
the story Ive heard with my ear to your belly,
a seashell history of evolution personified.

Your womb is a room where it's always afternoon.

The Night Before Michael Was Born

The picture is simply chile relleno,
chicken enchilada, refried beans &
rice with lettuce salad, cold beer

by the plainest doorway, cropping out
a vanishing world we never fit into
nor of which we've ever been fans.

It's warm in here but cold outside.
Our nervous feet touch under the table.
Can the baby inside you take hot sauce?

Studio up over In Your Ear

The radiator's hissing hot
My Smith-Corona's cleaned & oiled
with a fresh nylon ribbon
for the hard miles ahead

Gurney Norman's notes for his book
scribbled against this flaking wall
painted landlord green grow more
cryptic as the nights wear on
This used to be his working place

The sky over University Avenue
from my second-story window is
clean, calm, & black again in this
sudden warm night in December

Sleepily my inner voice thins
as, entering my characters' worlds,
I see all of life as unedited film
with no title, no lion, no Paramount
spangle of stars to soften what's ended,
altho everybody gets in on the credits

Far away, in the cabaret downstairs,
Asleep at the Wheel (a western country band)
breaks em up as their loud lead singer,
a little brunette with Woolworth's
in her voice, belts out, "You wanna
                        take me for a ride in the
                        backseat of your cawrr!"

Out on the sidewalk just below my half-
opened window three young men split
a fifth of Bali Hai & shoot the shit
& some craps 1940s-style to the music

Up here in free-lance heaven
Ive got my own floating game going on

The ante is tremendous & side bets
are OK, but youre lucky if you walk out
with the clothes on your back

December 26, 1972
Palo Alto, California
written three nights
before the cabaret
In Your Ear burned down

Not Her, She Aint No Gypsy

Fifteen years up & her tongue's still flapping
She lives in the calcium of her bones
She lives in the toughness of her liver
She lives in the memory of men she's made happy by surprise
That's her salvation for now, for the weekend

She raised a son this way but she wont get to heaven
Her heaven's got jukeboxes anyway
Lots of jukeboxes & well-peppered shot glasses, a little bush on the side, coin
    telephones
Her son's a nice kid, digs cars & girls & unh-hunh the North Pole, collects
    books & articles on it & secretly hopes to visit it
Just another almost American boy with a mixed-up sisterly mom

She was beautiful once, a wild way-out kid (as they said in those days) who'd
    try anything once, twice if it was nice enough
She's still beautiful in another kind of way
But she dont know this just yet
All she know is she still got ice & a lotta drink left & the happy-headed dude
    across the table say he just sold a tune to some rock band & they threw in

79

a little coke to boot so drink up love there's plenny more where this is
coming from

She gets high to connect with ecstasy & pretty soon before she know it
everything gets to be all elemental
Even as she pulls her panties up & kisses old hairy what's-his-name good
morning she still dont know just what it is that's been bugging her all
this time & how come her boy turned out so straight

But that's how it go
That's just how it go
She wouldnt change now, she couldnt come down for all the pills in Beverly
Hills, for all the booze in Veracruz

She aint sold out yet & her tongue's still flapping

Rediscovered Diary Entry

A glass of sweet milk
(stirred with honey)
warm by my cold Underwood

There's a woman asleep in my bed

Today I gorged myself on ice cream
& said several prayers
for energy to continue

Today I shook hands formally with
an old robed Zen master from Japan
whose head glistened youthfully
like the skin of a new golden apple
rubbed lovingly against a sleeve

Too many Aprils ago we
boarded the same bus mornings
in Berkeley with its plum blossoms
I would be on my way to work
He would simply be on his way
Today our fresh paths touched

Breathing before the pale wall of
my tiny writing room tonight,
I dissolve into all of the magazine
cutouts Ive carefully put up
to remind myself how lonely I am

Sleep must wait until daylight now
when the lady will leave for work
& I will already have done mine

Tonight in silence I sip my milk &
salute the snoring of the radiator

Today I am on my way

Visiting Day

for Conyus

This being a minimum security facility, it feels more like being on a reservation
than in a touchable cage

Books are allowed, smiles, eats (you could slip a .38 inside a baked chicken or a
file inside a loaf of sourdough french easily enough, but there's really not
much to shoot or saw thru)

You sign up, take a seat at one of the open-air picnic tables, & yawn from
hours of driving into the beautiful chilled morning

All the black inmates trudging by or hanging out of barracks windows give
you the power salute as you consider yourself again strapped down in their
skins

You walk, you talk, you toy around with words, you steal guarded looks down
into one another

A little food, fruit juice, a lot of gossip, & the sun on the trees under blue sky
surrounding us is magnified into one big silly-looking halo

"I'm not into meat all that much anymore, man, & there's a whole lotsa books
I wanna talk about &—here, these're some things I wrote last month—
thinking about that last letter I wrote you where I said my head was
getting peaceful—what's the bloods on the block woofing about these
days?"

He looks healthier than he did in the old macrobiotic city yogi wild bustling
days when you'd both get zonked on sounds in the middle of the
afternoon & reminisce for midnights about stuff that probably never
happened

This is what's known as a conservation camp where you cut & prune trees, dig
up the earth, seed the ground, weather watch, sweat a lot, do a little
basketball, sun on the run, sneak peeks at crotch shots in magazines
smuggled in from outside

You think of his woman, you think of his son, you think of them holed up
alone in the city, waiting & waiting for him to come home

You think of all the professionals involved: pipe smokers with advanced degrees
from state colleges—penologists, criminologists, sociologists who
minored in deviate psychology; in clean, classy ghettos where they never
take walks, their children snort coke on an allowance

Three tables away from where you sit consoling one another, a slim young man up on a burglary rap is splitting his attention between a 2-year-old daughter & a 22-year-old wife who's shown up thoughtfully in tight-fitted jeans ripped generously enough to allow him to see what she hasn't bothered wearing

Well, it isnt San Quentin, it isnt Attica, & it's no one's official prisoner of war camp, yet you cant help thinking there's a battle going on somewhere out there in the bloodstreams of men

You say good-bye, you shake hands good-bye, you stare good-bye; you wave what you havent said, you grin what you cannot say, you walk away & turn again to wave what neither of you has to say

You gun your engine good-bye & roar off down the California road back out into your own special prison

Weeks later you hear about the steel file some white inmate's driven into the heart of another white inmate found by your friend by some bushes in the rain—dead—because he was your friend's good friend, because he was a nigger lover, a nigger lover

The news chills the tips of your fingers & you sweat

Could it have been the father of the sweet little girl, husband of the gal whose ass was showing?

Could it have been the marijuana dealer who read the *Bhagavad Gita* & meditated nightly?

Could it have been the crinkly eyed loser who made you laugh & laugh when he talked about his life inside & outside the joint like a stand-up comic?

You think about the first person you ever screamed at

You think about the first thing you ever stole, or lied about, or killed

Green Is a Feeling, Not a Color

In the branches of your nerves
a draft passes, as in sleep
in a storm, as the tree bends
in nights no Columbus could sail

In summer an apple shines hollow
with many suns inside it, dreaming
women swimming slowly sandy shores
in green & yellow, bikinis that smile

There's nothing new here, just
an ancient new world: a picture of
stones & flesh slipping into an ocean
into chilled kisses, caresses, as a
child would a boot or carousel spinning
with flashing pink tongues, warm teeth

Leaves of your body are flying away,
original birds, flat without mouths,
out to backyards away from the sea
across dream sand the color of burnt snow

In the branches of your nerves
leaves must only be extensions of
all our trembling treeflesh, starflesh,
the body with arms held out, a star,
five-pointed, perfect to hang space
around or light for leaf or galaxy

Love, I feel you leafless, a field
the greenness of my own invention

Moss

The Rolling Stones,
a hard English group,
busted for heroin
at their Southern France estate,
fifty grams of smack a week
said the man on the news
just to keep
their little family extended

Well, so what,
whatll happen to them?
So what if the air
back of these superstars
gets waved away
from time to time
like those costly backdrops
in the old film factories?

Charles Christopher Parker,
a genius among geniuses,
was granted diplomatic immunity
the moment that he died

Eleanora Fagan Gough
(the Billie Holiday who now
powers many a Silver Cloud)
was a sufferer among sufferers
with narks up in her deathbed

Even Bela Lugosi,
our beloved Transylvanian,
sustained his habit in real life
& metaphorically on screen

Ah the Rolling Stones,
a hard English group,
heroes of an American era

Demerol

The glamour of this moment too will pass.
This bright warm wind that whispers thru me now,
thru my body, a dwelling place of spirit,
will blow itself away.

                              Like laughing gas
that dentists used in 1910 for pain,
this sweet drug even now feels out-of-date.
Is it their muzak oozing from the walls,
crisp leaves of city trees quivering with rain
outside this clinic window where I lie
that make me sad & at the same time feel
that I could swim this sinking stream of joy
forever?——no how-are-you, no good-bye.

Delicious as it seems, it doesnt last.
Having to do it over & over again
means keeping up with Joneses that dont die.

American Glamour

Is my dress appropriate?
Is my breath still fresh?
Will my underarms fail me?
What about my hair?
Should I have gotten it shaped,
is it long enough
to proclaim to one & all
my true & lasting blackness?

It's the 7 a.m. flight.
Even the plane seems to yawn
as they test its engines
one by one in the historic fog of
San Francisco International.

The stewardesses in their
miniskirted uniforms,
designed by some promotional committee
to make them look pretty & sexy,
look silly, look shot, look
O so American cheesecake!

There arent enough minutes
between now & landing to
savor these ridiculous niceties:
coffee in flight, token sweet roll,
documentary voice of the pilot
droning the time, temperatures,
                    altitudes, cruising speeds. . . .

Dozing amid commuters who'd fall
into deep sleep if they only knew
they were up here with a poet
trying to play his nuttiness down,
I'm on my way to interview
the great Ray Charles on assignment.

Pacific Southwest Airlines into L.A. today
—tomorrow? Who knows? Trans World!

Roland Navarro (1939–1961)

I leave you on that downtown street of
how many Detroit winters ago, standing
in front of the March of Dimes display
in a window, wincing aloud to me of suffering
people all over the world where a boy
cut out of cardboard on crutches implores,
"Please won't you help? Please won't you give?"

You were home from West Point, the holidays,
still owing me a big bottle of vodka from
some high-school bet that's as dark & forgotten
as any old joke from the shadowy past.

You wanted to be a big general down in
South America, Argentina, where your skilled dad
took refuge after twenty years of visiting you
weekends at his parents' home, your grand-
parents' house on Clairmount not far from
12th Street where we each caught buses, sometimes
together, & lived straight out of our heads
littered with print, pictures, & old pianos—
you Chicano, me black, both of us niggers.

We loved the same girls more than once & you
wrote in a letter how I should think twice
about becoming a poet or artist of any kind
because the mad world had no more need of
that kind of craziness: *"They grind you down
and fuck you around, then toss you a crumb or
a well-gnawed bone, then shit on you again."*
You told me, *"Be a soldier, be an ass kicker,
& get in on the take by starting at the top."*

How many times we played your Napoleon game
with paper ships & troops in war-torn Novembers!
Cursing like a sailor, upsetting my mother,
you wrote enough of an epic novel to impress
the hell out of me along with your drawings
& that piano piece of yours called *Funeral Bells*.
I still have the portrait you did of me when
I was studying trumpet— *Young Horn with a Boy*.

So your father remarried, a woman more our age,
leaving you with snapshots of your mother,
a legend who died before you'd learned to love.
I leave you watery-eyed in front of that paper
publicity cripple, you who wanted to rule men
tall in your shiny black Argentine boots,
frightened by a tenderness your heart couldnt rule.
Here the world ends, here the sun's hidden
forever from a scene you abandoned slyly
to return to your bright new Connecticut love
whose photo you flashed reminded me of
your lost mama & a princess named Juanita
(uncrowned object of our junior-high search)
but this sure-enough Her Highness was rich
& fair.
        Come that summer you'd finally marry
the goddess you always accused me of seeking.

You did it, you did it, you outfoxed fate!
You survived the honor system & graduated clean.
I looked forward to studying you in histories
to come but the world & impatience got in the way.
All that Pérez Prado we'd been thru together,
all that Mingus, Debussy, *Swan Lake* & the Penguins,
Rimbaud, Charlie Parker, Tolstoi, Cézanne, Joe Loco
wasn't enough to head off an ending I'd rather
imagine than know as I did Vivian or Nina,
as I know the moon of honey Mexico where you died
in an auto crash that killed you outright &
left your bride crippled like that poster child.

I think of you always, I even hum your song
here where what's right must collide with what's wrong.

1961–1973

Ho

She coulda been somethin
like the Supremes or somebody
Her folks give her everything she need
I use to know her family pretty good
They dont have that much but they
        aint on relief
She call herself in love

Her money it go for that stuff, I guess,
        & for strong mouthwash, I know
I see her buyin Baby Ruths & Twinkies too
        down at the liquor store

Every night she start her day
right under my window when the lights
        come on
She aint bad-lookin neither, just little

She just a skinny little sister
bout big as my fist
but even she done slipped & found out
heaven aint the only H in the dictionary

Making Love After Hours

Back up in the room they snap on
all-nite movies but leave the sound
turned down, turned off.
                You see,
neon & smoke last just so long & soon
there're no more joints to haunt
or get lost in, no more ghosts to give up

except the flicker & ripple of TV light
against their shot bodies quivering with shadow.

With an urgency of children permitted to
stay up way past bedtime, they share,
they linger, they nurse the last drink.
They whisper & they whisper, sighing to collapse.

She peels off her turtleneck,
undoes her jeans, kicks her sandals
straight toward the window as the moon comes up
shining thru clouds in a rainy 1930s
tight-suit movie, too mellow a moon,
like some yawning display in a budget-store window.

For weeks & weeks he's dragged around feeling
sorry for himself but now unalone, naked
next to her, he just cant remember how much
                    or how come.

Two stories down, drunks stumble the streets
in search of some phone booths to pee in.

"Boogie with O. O. Gabugah"

Note -

O.O. Gabugah writes that he "was born in a taxicab right smack
on 125th and Lenox in Harlem on Lincoln's Birthday, 1945.
Franklin Delano Watson was the name my poor brainwashed parents
gave me but I had that racist tag legally altered once I got old
enough to see what was going down. The O.O., by the way, stands
for Our Own, i.e., we need to do *our own* thing, can you dig it?"

In addition to being one of our strongest young Black revolutionary
voices, Brother Gabugah is the author of half a dozen volumes,
all of which have appeared since last year. *Slaughter the Pig &
Git Yo'self Some Chit'lins* is the title of his most popular work
which is presently in its sixth big printing. Other volumes
include: *Niggers with Knives, Black on Back, Love Is a White
Man's Snot-Rag* and *Takin Names and Kickin Asses.* His plays—
Transistor Willie & Latrine Lil and *Go All the Way Down & Come
Up Shakin* (a revolutionary Black musical)—received last month's
Drama Authority Award.

The brother is presently the recipient of both a Federal Arts
Agency grant as well as a Vanderbilt Fellowship to conduct research
on Richard Wright. Currently vacationing in Australia, he is
preparing a collection of critical essays tentatively titled
Woodpile Findings: Cultural Investigations into What's Goin On.

His last critical work, *Nothin Niggers Do Will Ever Please Me,*
is also a favorite.

"O.O. Gabugah draws strong folk poetry from the voice of a strident
but vital revolutionary who attacks the Uncle Tom," states
The Nation in its March 19, 1973 issue.

A militant advocate of the oral tradition, he chooses to dictate
his poems through me rather than write them down himself.

The Old O. O. Blues

Like right now it's the summertime
    and I'm so all alone
I gots to blow some fonky rhyme
    on my mental saxophone

Brother Trane done did his thang
    and so have Wes Montgomery,
both heavyweights in the music rang,
    now I'mo play my summary

It's lotsa yall that thank yall white
    (ought I say European?)
who thank Mozart and Bach's all right,
    denyin your Black bein

Well, honkyphiles, yall's day done come,
    I mean we gon clean house
and rid the earth of Oreo scum
    that put down Fats for Faust

This here's one for-real revolution
    where aint nobody playin
We intends to stop this cultural pollution
    Can yall git to what I'm sayin?

Sittin up here in your Dior gown
    and Pierre Cardin suit
downtown where all them devil clowns
    hang out and they aint poot!

We take the white man's bread and grants
    but do our own thang with it
while yall bees itchin to git in they pants
    and taint the true Black spirit

I'm blowin for Bird and Dinah and Billie,
    for Satch, Sam Cooke, and Otis,
for Clifford, Eric, and Trane outta Philly
    who split on moment's notice

Chump, you aint gon never change,
    your narrow ass is sankin
Like Watergate, your shit is strange
    You drownin while we thankin

My simple song might not have class
    but you cant listen with impunity
We out to smash your bourgeois ass
    and by *we* I mean The Community!

Black Queen for More Than a Day

I thirst for
      the Kool-Aid
  of your fabulous
fine fruit-flavored throat

Lick that ebony tongue
      out at me
    and let that licorice
    divine heavenly lickrish
      slide down my system

Chocolate mama, *mmm mmm*

Beauty is to boodie as
      class struggle is
        to ass struggle
    so let's git it on
  for the night is long

When you place your hot dark arm
    cross my chest
      I'm like
  some fierce tribal warrior
    ready to git
  down to natural bizness

With my head held high
  I walk through the sky
      with its cornrow of stars
  and you scroonched all
    up next to me
      sweet as you are

I'm the original poet
  (and I damn well know it)
    when you suckle me,
      you stallion you

Black woman
  my African Queen
    for more than a day
  kiss me with your
    Congo
      lips

What You Seize Is What You Git

You must thank
        yo dookey don't stank
            while you be's gittin high
                up in the sky
    of yo hand-
                ker-
                        chief
                            head
                                home, nigga,
        you sorryass muthafucka,
    swillin slop at the white beast's
                            trough
            (like black aint down enough),
            payin taxes insteada
                grindin axes,
            slurpin up all that Boone's Farm
                Strawberry Hill
(oughta be called hell)
                    wine,
                you wind-up computerized
                    Sambo

    •You look like somethin
            outta Tarzan
    just can't wait to sniff Jane's titty,
            thinkin you pretty,
        but you aint nothin, nigga,
        you and yo old lady workin
            4 jobs 7 days a week
                & wont even speak
                up for yo rights
                    day or nite
                just so yo pickaninny chile
                    can grow up and run the mile
                    in the racist Olympics,
                oil for yall to slide for a ride
                        on into the middle class

Well, all yall can kiss my revolutionary ass!

We tireda niggas buyin Cholly's wine and cars
      and neckties and bell-bottoms and yes books
      and bein bused to his plastic schools
      to learn how to be some white kinda fool

We talkin bout hackin the bleached-out devil
         to pieces
         & shippin Chunks-O-Hunky out to Venus
           for the interplanetary brothers
               up there to chew on, muthas,
            you sassyass beautiful black muthas
               tryin to fare well on welfare

Quit playin with yo'self, nigga, & come!
    Come on back into the warm black fold
    that aint got nothin to do with gold!

Come on back where we at and *live*, i.e.,
    lib-er-rated, de-*live*-ered
            from tyranny!

Come on back where we rezides
    greaze on some greens
    and check some sides—

        Shoot ol Pharoah
        (and we dont mean Brothers Sanders)
          in the butt with yo poisoned Kikuyu arrow
        unless you tryna be the knee-grow Ann Landers . . .

        It still aint too late
        to keep the fate, Gate!

        Write on, Bruh,
        with yo funky baaaaad-ass
        Afro-headed
          self!

                           Paris/Dar-es-Salaam
                           1972

A Poem for Players

Yes, theyll let you play,
let you play third base or fender bass,
let you play Harrah's Club or Shea Stadium

Theyll let you play
in a play anyway: Shakespeare,
Ionesco, Bullins, Baraka, or Genet,
only dont get down *too* much
& dont go gettin too uppity

Theyll let you play,
oh yes, on the radio, stereo,
even on the video, Ojays,
O.J. Simpson, only please dont stray
too far from your ghetto rodeo

Theyll let you be Satchmo,
theyll let you be Diz,
theyll let you be Romeo,
        or star in *The Wiz*
but you gots to remember that
        that's all there is

Oh, you can be a lawyer or a medico,
a well-briefcased executive with Texaco;
you can even get yourself hired, man,
to go teach *Ulysses* in Dublin, Ireland

Theyll let you play
so long as you dont play around,
so long as you play it hot or cool,
so long as you dont play down the blues
theyll let you play in *Playboy*, *Playgirl*,
or the *Amsterdam News*

Finally theyll let you play
politics if you dont get in the way
some of us did and had to be
iced by conspiracy, international mystery

Theyll let you play anybody but you,
that's pretty much what they will do

East Boston

for Denise Levertov

Up in this warm, solid house of yours
while you make breakfast I stand sighing
at the window, breaths away from
this working-class block where trash cans
lined up in front of old buildings
look natural with sun shining down on them

If my heart seems to leap from my shirt
away away away from this instant it's
because the short drive in from Logan Airport
thru last night's minute of neighborhood
streetlight with children playing in it
is whisking me back thru my decades again

Way past dark we chased one another
We had our own style of stickball too
when the England you smiled in wasnt so new

If my voice is quivering it's also because
the sky up over your Boston Inner Harbor
is too splendid to look at this morning—
cool waters below, those barges so sober!

Ive lived for so long now on another coast

Providence, Rhode Island

It's spring again
the early part when
the wettest wind
gives you a licking
youll never forget

You stand quivering
down by the Biltmore
whistling for taxis
as maxiskirted women
flee the scene
youve just stepped into

The grayness of this
white water city feels
good to blood that wants
to explode on century's notice
shattering calendar meat
& appointments well kept

Colonial afternoons
had to be colder than
the hearts of witches
laid to rest beneath
these charming city paved hills

Rushing for cover
you now understand the
cooled-out literalness
of these old wooden homes

A skinny black man
(a brother you guess)
who commutes between
this stop & Harlem U.S.A.
tells you he's never been to
Brown or the School of Design
but he know for a fact that
it's Mafia keep this town relaxed

"They got the highest houses
up in them hills but after them
come all your professors & pro-
fessionals, people with a
high-class license to steal"

You want to come back in
summer when the change takes
place but this brilliant chill
has tightened your head

New England is a poker game too

New Orleans Intermission

*"A lighted window holds me like
high voltage. I see . . ."*
    Walter Benton
    This Is My Beloved

I

I see it zooming down
over the bayou late April
morning of the brightest green
from the window of a jet named Nancy

Settling back childishly
in the sky all alone,
my secret hand waves light aside
to get a better look at
all the music coiling up

inside me again as I watch
this still virgin landscape

Is that the famous Mississippi
down there, are those the streets
Jelly Roll did his marching,
strutting, & poolsharking in?
Was I really just born
a gulf away from here or
carved like Pinocchio
from some thick dark tree below?

2

The only way to love a city's
to live in it till you know
every door every store every
parkingmeter deadlawn alleycat
district smell pussy hotel
gumwrapper & wino by heart

Airborne all night my sleepy heart
leaps like windblown raindrops
I'm a very old baby reentering
an unchanged world with a yawn

3

Yes Ive lived here before
just as I know & can feel in my tongue
that Ive tramped this earth as
storyteller & unaccountable thief
too many times before,
a displaced lover of spirit & flesh

Riding the St. Charles trolley nights
an old American, classically black,
spots me as a tourist & softly explains
how he dont have to take snapshots
no more since he can more or less
picture in his mind what's keepable

When I take this 15¢ ride, the cool
off-hour breeze tightening my skin,
I can tune in to people telling their
stories real slow in the form of asides
& catch myself doing a lot of smiling
to hold back tears

        Old-timer tells me
why the fare on this line's so cheap:
"It's so the colored maids & cooks &
gardeners can git to they jobs & back
without it bein a strain on they pocket"

4

On Bourbon Street (North Beach or
Times Square) a fan-tailed redhead in
G-string & nothing else waves me
into a topless/bottomless joint with a
dog-faced barker posted at the door
who yips & howls: "C'mon in yall & see
southron gals takin off they draws
for just the price of a drink!"
        It isnt
enough to laugh & rush in like a
prospective drunk that's in heat
The point is that love & love alone
holds up my feet as they step from
Bourbon to Rampart Street, dreaming of
Congo Square, Creole intrigue, Fats
Domino & Dr. John while a black panhandler
(cross between Satchmo & Papa John Creach)
hits on me for 50¢ in front of Al Hirt's

5

Steaming hot down in front of us now:
ham biscuit eggs grits Cajun coffee
& a solid glass of buttermilk for me
for fun—

It's Mama's in the morning
where American poet Miller Williams
leans past his dark wife, Becky, to say:
"You probly the only Californian that
really knows about this place, man"

I know I'll slip back by for gumbo,
for lunch known down here as dinner,
or for a supper of 90¢ crawfish bisque

But right now it's the light quivering
in from the street down onto our plates
that makes us quit talking poetry

"I'd give up writing," Miller sighs,
"if I could sing as good as Ray Charles"

Tomorrow theyll drive back to the Ozarks
Tomorrow I'll fly back to California
where there're no nickel phone calls,
pick up the show from where I left off
& read Marie Laveau the Voodoo Queen

City Home/Detroit

Old emotions like powdery tenements
undulate in the July heat
It would take an ocean of sentiment
to cool your memories of this street
that first contained your notions of how
the world operates, how it is what it is.

How your body sweats & pours now
as it prepares to deal with the quiz

that's been haunting you all these years
of walking the earth, stepping thru time,
refining your eyesight, opening your ears
for a liberating music, scales you can climb.

What if you never had run from this race
(Cleveland to Detroit to Chicago, New York)?
What if you'd settled & stayed in your place
among friends who'd never arrive at that fork
in the road of their flat midwestern lives
where Atlantic & Pacific equals A & P,
where rock salt's for winter, & when summer arrives
wish for showers to ease the humidity?

In your California sandals & flowery shirt,
hair a juicy network of coils & strands,
hoping today you wont get robbed or hurt,
you know what forced you to seek other lands.

Dude in Denver

This skinny little dude
up next to a mountain
(the Rockies, eastern slope)
with his wimp mouth look,
cap not even fitting
his pointed head right

His lips hang out from his
mouth & kinda to one side
so when he talk they flap
just enough so you can spot him
from grand distances

He takes a sip of 7Up
from a can swiped from a truck,
adjusts the floppy collar of
his leather coat & Big Apple cap,
blinks behind winter shades
as a cold-blooded Lincoln snores by

Skied over, he undergoes a change
of nerve, looking over both shoulders
to make sure no one's watching
before approaching the parked bike
left unlocked by some college-looking
white girl who could show up any
minute to blow the whistle for good
on this good thing he thinks he's got

Oppression? Repression? Suppression?
Depression? The pressure he's under,
were it ever let out, might heat up
this windblown November afternoon

Can he really be as sad as he looks
now, hunched over in need of a ten-speed
bicycle, cheerless, thin, a thief so
leery of anything passing in the light
within reach of his wet, greedy eyes?—

A Colorado colored boy, Afro, American,
a downright American little dude

California Peninsula: El Camino Real

In 15 minutes
the whole scene'll change
as bloated housewives
hems of their skirts greased
with love mouths wide open
come running out of shops
dragging their young
moon in their eyes
the fear upon them

Any minute now
the gas-blue sky over El Camino Real
is going to droop for good
shut with a squish &
close them all in like
a giant irritated eye

Theyll scramble for cars
the nearest road out
clutching their steering wheels
like stalwart monkeys

It couldve happened yesterday
It couldve happened while they
were sighing in Macy's Walgreen's 31 Flavors
Copenhagen Movies or visiting the Colonel
like that earthquake night
that shattered L.A.

Whatll they will their children then?
Whatll they leave for them to detest?
What tree, what lip print, what Jack in
what Box, what ugly hot order to go?

Already I can smell the darkness
creeping in like the familiar shadow
of some beloved fake monster
in a science fiction flick

In 15 minutes
48 hours days weeks months
years from now all of thisll be
a drowsy memory barely tellable
in a land whose novelty was speech

Geography of the Near Past

The trick
without anyone's
catching on to it
is to swim against
world current
knowing it to be as much a dream
as it is drama on the highest stage
but without losing touch
with spirit or with light

Realer even
is to move as if
nothing has ever happened
which is likewise
as true as foam or fog

Each universe is only
an ever-shifting sea
in the surfacing eyes of former fish

Teaching

There's no such thing as a student,
only abiding faces unwilling
to change except with time,
the oldest force that still fools us

So you teach a feeling,
a notion learned the hard way,
a fact, some figures,
a tract, some rigors of childhood

The face out there
interacting with yours
knows how to grin & play with its pen
but misses the point so charmingly

A thousand moves later
that same shiny face
moving thru the world with
its eyes glazed or fully closed
reconnects with one of its own childhoods

Loosely we call this learning

Aunt

She talks too loud, her face
a blur of wrinkles & sunshine
where her hard hair shivers
from laughter like a pine tree
stiff with oil & hotcombing

O & her anger realer than gasoline
slung into fire or lighted mohair
She's a clothes lover from way back

108

but her body's too big to be chic
or on cue so she wear what she want
People just gotta stand back &
take it like they do Easter Sunday when
the rainbow she travels is dry-cleaned

She laughs more than ever in spring
stomping the downtowns, Saturday past
work, looking into JC Penney's checking
out Sears & bragging about how when she
feel like it she gon lose weight &
give up smokin one of these sorry days

Her eyes are diamonds of pure dark space
& the air flying out of them as you look
close is only the essence of living
to tell, a full-length woman, an aunt
brown & red with stalking the years

Poetry

It is possible to rest here.
It is possible to arrive home
headed this way
thru the wind & rain of this night
alone
to a place where starlight
isnt the point.
It is true that we are orphans
under the skin
where fluids combine
& organisms function intelligently,

where vision or sound
in image or vibration
need only be true
to spark the way there.
There is here & always was.
You sniff & clear your throat
in this unintentional night
borrowed from eternity
or let yourself be saddened by nothing.
I sit in a white kitchen
next to the young walls,
yellow paper spread on yellow tablecloth,
& scratch helplessly,
wanting to take new leave
of the present
which was a gift,
longing to have known everything
& to have been everywhere
before the world dissolves
a tangle of journeys
& messages
unrecorded
undeciphered
wrinkled down into me.

The Blues Don't Change

How the Rainbow Works

for Jean Cook, on learning of her mother's death

Mostly we occupy ocular zones, clinging
only to what we think we can see.
We can't see wind or waves of thought,
electrical fields or atoms dancing;
only what they do or make us believe.

Look on all of life as color—
vibratile movement, heart-centered,
from invisibility to the merely visible.
Never mind what happens when one of us dies.
Where are you before you even get born?
Where am I and all the unseeable souls
we love at this moment, or loathed
before birth? Where are we right now?

Everything that ever happened either
never did or always will with variations.
Let's put it another way: Nothing ever
happened that wasn't dreamed, that wasn't
sketched from the start with artful surprises.
Think of the dreamer as God, a painter,
a ham, to be sure, but a divine old master
whose medium is light and who sidesteps
tedium by leaving room both inside and outside
this picture for subjects and scenery to wing it.

Look on death as living color too: the dyeing
of fabric, submersion into a temporary sea,
a spectruming beyond the reach of sensual
range which, like time, is chained to change;
the strange notion that everything we've
ever done or been up until now is past
history, is gone away, is bleached, bereft,
perfect, leaving the scene clean to freshen
with pigment and space and leftover light.

Michael at Sixteen Months

Ball	His whole world revolves around light dark
Bird	things sailing thru the air around chairs
Dog	the mystery of rising & falling & getting
Cheese	up again in the morning at night/scratching
Shoes	at windows to get out bananas oranges a
Cat	step/stepping down stepping up/keep the music
Juice	going/TV theme songs/walks on stones, dancing
Baby	on manhole covers, anything circular, objects
Daddy	that hang & flap in the breeze/the wind as
Mama	it foams into a room making the skin cool
Boat	puffing out curtains/baths/water/legs/kiss
Mama	Here we go into the rain turning sunlight
	Here we go down the slide into sandpiles
Mommy	Here we go clapping our hands as blocks fall
	Here we go running from Mama Mommy Mimi baby
No	crashing into Daddy dozing on the floor, a
	world is shooting out of rubber tree leaves
Nose	The window is a magic mirror/sad to see time
	flowing throwing itself thru flesh electric
Hot	that hard months ago was only a flash in
	a sea of possibility/the suffering afloat
Car	The meanness he will have to endure is only
	life ungathered in the eye of no world/is light
Book	pure & not so simple after all is living life
	alive alive O!

A Sleepy Day at Half Moon Bay

Like the shark who feels low but
frequent sound waves from afar
telling him it's dinnertime
somewhere under the sea,
I feel the pull of waves
splashing from my own center,
  softly, slowly—
lapping at my insides like a
long-forgotten dream that pops up
changed around years later,
more familiar & realer than noon

Ars Poetica

"All that we did was human,
  stupid, easily forgiven,
Not quite right."
  Gary Snyder

Now that nothing has worked out
and the beautiful trees
are again in winter, feeding
on lean November light; the world,
like the cold, tentative and tight
around his skin, his heart about
to pound right out of him,
he can linger on this corner again,
unnoticed, another dude in another street,
waiting for someone to keep an appointment
in the frozen belly of a large city,
no string quartets, no studio brass
bands to grace the meaningless background,

only the warmth of personal sun,
a blossoming peace stretching out.
In the soft folds of his brain—
she arrives as in a living photograph,
her everyday breath steaming the air,
warm under coat and sweater, simple
skirt, boots, the colored elastic of
her pants underneath snapped snugly
into place at the waist, at the thigh.

Poem with Orange

Finally you sit
at some table and put
your little life back
together again by
slicing a new orange

How closely the wet
glistening flesh of
this bright cut fruit
reassembles all galaxies

How comfortably its
sweet pattern fits yours
as you watch each matching
diamond-juiced wedge
reaching, edging toward
essence, the center, home

Fort Collins, Colorado

for Mary Crow

The present is a gift,
the past just a shift
in perspective balanced on thin air,
time sat out in a rocking chair

Neither of us knew those men
who made themselves at home here when
sky wasn't for sale and Denver
was a clean high clearing closeby, remember?

People of Letters

The mystery here in this paperweight world
is that anything of beauty gets written at all.
If poets are the unacknowledged legislators
of the world, then give me Benito Mussolini
who, tyrant though he was, made the trains run
on time, produced a bebop piano-playing son
and had no need of a penny-wise poet apologist.

Literary affairs may be likened to county fairs
or state fairs; theatrical events, the bigger
the badder, with carnival rides, bristling midways,
prize livestock, quilting bees, orchid displays,
pickled music, hot buttered corn and action booths
for streamered Chamber of Commerce concessions.
Unbusinesslike lovers of life had best just visit.

Foggy Morning

Disappearing around the corner
in his nylon red jacket with
the hood slipping from his hair
just brushed, my son trailing
gladness through clouds on the ground
waving to me that he can see the
yellow bus waiting for him up
ahead. Clutching his book, waving,
waving, with nothing but life.
I stand on the porch waving back,
a lump in my throat from moving
through the fog of my years that
sunshine is destined to dissolve.

New Autumn, New York

Late in the day when light is sandwiched
softly between slices of daytime and night,
I stroll around Gramercy Park, locked as usual
and all keyed up again for the real autumn.

To the falling of leaves in time-lapse slow
motion, I follow my feet, each crackling step
nudging me into a vaster present than this
friendly seasonal chill can circumscribe.

There is no end to the inward adventure of
journeying October to the edge of November.

A Little Poem About Jazz

for Miles Davis

Sometimes at the beginning of a movie
when they're flashing the title and heavy
credits over aerial shots of old New York—
skyscrapers that aren't really skyscrapers
because you'd have to be miles high to
see them that way on an everyday basis—
I think about *Green Dolphin Street* blown
over with wind and sound, and I picture
Elizabeth Goudge, whatever she looked like,
up on the stand with you, Trane and Cannonball,
a flower in her hair, a song in her throat.

The Art of Benny Carter

There are afternoons in jazz
when a leaf turns and falls
with so much barely noticed purity
that the not so secret meaning of
everything men and women have
tried to do beyond keeping afloat
becomes as clear as ocean air.

Intimacy

Right up under our noses, roses
arrive at middleage, cancer blooms
and the sea is awash with answers.

Right here where light is brightest,
we sleep deepest; ignorant dreamers
with the appetites of napping apes.

Right this way to the mystery of life!
Follow your nose, follow the sun or
follow the dreaming sea, but follow!

Chemistry

What connects me to this moon
is legendary, and what connects
. the moon to me is as
momentary as the night is
long before it burns away like
that fire in the eyes of lovers
when, spent, they turn
from one another and fall against
the dark sides of their pillows
to let their blood color cool.

You too know well the nature of
our chemistry: 65% oxygen,
18% carbon, 10% hydrogen,
3% nitrogen, a touch of calcium,
phosphorous and other elements.
But largely (by 70%) we're water:
2 parts hydrogen to 1 part oxygen,
and mostly we're still all wet—

9 parts fear chained to 1 part joy.
Is this why we're given to drowning
ourselves in pools of tears,
long on sorrow and shallow on laughter;
drowning ourselves in sugar and salt
as it were, as we are, as the treasured
substance of a former fish's life
can never be technically measured?

This chemistry we swim and skim
is what connects all light with me
olympically, for real life
science will forever be proving
this radiant suspension to be love
in but one of its bubbling mutations.

Billie

Music: a pattern etched into time

I suck on my lemon, I squeeze my lime
into a bright but heady drink, soft
to the tongue, cold to touch, and wait

She who is singing enters my mouth,
a portion at a time: an arm, a leg,
a nipple, an eye, strands of hair—
There! Her song goes down and spins
around the way a toy pinwheel does, as
rosy blue blur, as rainbow, whirling
me through her throaty world and higher

Chug-a-lug enchantress, show me your
etchings. Warm me again now with
the red of your Cleopatric breath

In Marin Again

for Arl

Again we drift back to these mountains, these
divine inclines our son could scale now.
Your loose blouse blows as you lean in worn jeans,
making it easy, a breeze to picture your breasts
underneath, your long legs: time's salty hello
still freely flowing after years of rainfall.
Smoothly we slip into this renewable night of
jagged crossings over dark peaks, fitful, fruitful.

Like mountains and rivers that go on and on,
love growing wild is wondrous, isn't it, with
its crazy horse catch-as-catch-can way of proving
that happiness, after all, is mostly remembered?

Love on the move encircles itself, boomerangs,
rounding out meaning the way water smooths stone.

Mid-Life Crisis: A Critical Review

Of course you will always want to be
in places where you are loved, even in
the middle of life, even in darkness,
that restless spot where childhood and
youth (so used to looking after you)
collapse, leaving you as vulnerable to
change as the song where you turn into
a one-eyed cat peeping in a seafood store.

What you really want, all you really need
is everything, absolutely everything and
to be by yourself until this storm blows over.
Yet left alone, you quickly become like a
fully grown zebra, snatched from its habitat
and shipwrecked in a zoo, straightjacketed
in your own skin whose shadows and bright stripes
tiger the burning noons and nights you stalk
like a self-jailed cellmate, solitary, confined;
you the turncoat, you the turnkey; eye to eye
with yourself at last, tooth to soothing tooth.

A Sunday Sonnet for My Mother's Mother

for Mrs. Lillian Campbell

Consider her now, glowing, light-worn,
arthritic, crippled in a city backroom
far from the farm where she was born
when King Cotton was still in bloom.

She is as Southern as meat brown pecans,
or fried green tomato, or moon pies.

Gathering now for eight decades, aeons
of volunteered slavery soften her sighs.

Talk about somebody who's been there,
this grand lady has seen, remembers it all
and can tell you about anyone anywhere
in voices as musical as any bird's call.

Loving her, it hurts to hear her say,
"My grandchildren, they just threw me away."

Falling Asleep in a Darkening Room

Blue, the most beautiful of afternoons
is to lie transfixed with pressure brought
to bear on your dozing zone, and then to
feel air being let out of the giant world,
a balloon big enough to live on but not live in
except perhaps to sleepers dreaming they're awake.

To lay you down to sleep with winter blowing
through rooms where you've been worrying too much,
run your engine's battery down to barely audible
palm-held miniature radio level . . . *Shhhhh* . . .

Now you can let laughter bubble out of silence
like kindergarten blobs of color flung against *emptiness,*
emptiness; and let every unhurried passerby
become a painted shadow remembered in a slow dream
you always wanted to have, but haven't had yet,
not until now when, nodding, fading, you let go.

124

Everything you ever thought you were leaves you.
Alone, you wake up yesterday or maybe last week
or, fortunate, you fade back in, expanded again,
feeling virginal, refreshed—a new you not so blue.

W. H. Auden & Mantan Moreland

in memory of the Anglo-American poet & the Afro-American comic actor (famed
for his role as Birmingham Brown, chauffeur in those ancient Charlie
Chan movies) who died on the same day in 1973

Consider them both in paradise,
discussing one another—
the one a poet, the other an actor;
interchangeable performers
who finally slipped backstage
of a play whose cast favored lovers.

"You executed some brilliant lines,
Mr. Auden, & doubtless engaged our
innermost emotions & informed imagination,
for I pondered your *Age of Anxiety*
diligently over a juicy order of ribs."

"No shit!" groans Auden, mopping his brow.
"I checked out all your Charlie Chan
flicks & flipped when you turned up again
in *Watermelon Man* & that gas commercial
over TV. Like, where was you all that
time in between? I thought you'd done
died & gone back to England or somethin."

"Wystan, pray tell, why did you ever eliminate
that final line from 'September 1, 1939'?—
We must all love one another or die."

"That was easy. We gon die anyway no matter
how much we love, but the best thing I like
that you done was the way you buck them eyes
& make out like you runnin sked all the time.
Now, that's the bottom line of the black
experience where you be in charge of the scene.
For the same reason you probly stopped shufflin."

Going Back Home

The burros are all heehawed out
The rum is gone and our friends with it
—24 hours of pure loneliness
explained and joked and glanced away

The stars are out barking with the dogs
but flowers trees cornstalks and tomato
plants are fast asleep, chilled down in mist
We walk into town and argue and stare at
our cousins and nephews languishing in
produce stalls or under streetlamps in door-
ways and on the edges of taxi seats

Children play pinball and jockey machines,
their mothers and fathers clinking pesos
together late in the 20th Century mestizo night

We retreat to our lookout laid in the hills
with green invisibleness at this hour, down

our aspirin and vitamins B and C and walk
around the fireplace filled with wet wood,
newspaper and the dry hopes of the ages

With the aid of kerosene, soon there is
smoke rising up the chimney like light from
the village plaza below, reaching our window
with a choo-choo warmth as though there
were no such thing as Mexico or America,
only the lonely, naked spirits of people
shooting out of eyes and flesh, rambling
up these old mountains and back down again

What Is the Blues?

Far away, I suppose you could say,
is where I'm always coming back from.
In any event it's where I want to be
—naked, undressable, inaccessible,
at the tip edge of the vanishing point.

Of course I keep thinking of throwing   *metonymy*
in the towel but it isn't wet enough yet.
So, on a dare, I keep splashing around,
ducking down and coming up for air: my
tiny fair share of cool fulfillment.

And to vanish wouldn't be so bad.
Look at the visible, behold it slowly
and closely with unreddened eyes.
Without the stirrings of the heart
swimming in borrowed light, what could
we ever possibly lie down and see?

The James Cotton Band at Keystone

And the blues, I tell you, they blew up
on target; blew the roof right off
& went whistling skyward, starward,
stilling every zooming one of us
mojo'd in the room that night, that
instant, that whenever-it-was. Torn
inside at first, we all got turned out,
twisting in a blooming space where
afternoon & evening fused like Adam
with Eve. The joyful urge to cry
mushroomed into a blinding cloudburst
of spirit wired for sound, then atomized
into one long, thunderous, cooling downpour.

What ceased to be was now & now & now.
Time somehow was what the blues froze
tight like an underground pipe before
busting it loose in glad explosions; a
blast that shattered us—ice, flow & all.
The drift of what we'd been began to
shift, dragging us neither upstream nor
down but lifting us, safe & high, above
the very storm that, only flashing moments
ago, we'd been huddling in for warmth.

Melted at last, liquefied, we became
losers to the blues & victors, both.
Now that he'd blown us away with his shout,
this reigning brownskinned wizard, wise
to the ways of alchemy, squeezed new life
back into us by breathing through cracks
in our broken hearts; coaxing & choking
while speaking in tongues that fork & bend
like the watery peripheries of time; a
crime no more punishable than what the
dreaming volcano does waking from what it was.

Believe me, the blues can be volatile too,
but the blues don't bruise; they only renew.

Jungle Strut

Gene Ammons, 1969

Of all the nights, yours were greenest, Gene,
blue-breathing son of your boogie-bled dad
who, like you after him, left this dry world
a treasure tray of cocktails for the ear.

You loved making people high with your song
just as you must've loved soaring some yourself.
How high? Moon high, scaling neon heights like
an eagle humming along on silence and a bellyful.

Dumb hunters stalked you, staking you out shame-
lessly, especially when you were straddling air
pockets that, however turbulent, never blew away
your sound and rollicking command of flight.

The wine poured from your jug (when you weren't
locked up in one) was aging and tasty. Bottoms up!

My Spanish Heart

Chick Corea, 1977

In audible dreams I'm forever going back
to Spain. Now, tell me what that's all about?
Perhaps in some past life or lives I lived
there and cared about the African presence
in Iberia or New Iberia, eh? Get serious!
It's probably because all my life I've been
an all-nite sucker for spicy rhythm ticking
and booming away like an afro-latinized gypsy
taxi meter waiting to be fed that long mileage.

Whatever the reason or rhyme, I can think of
no better fate than to end up masking my nights
in the gardens of Spain—and how Spanish is
Spain?—with a warm, bubbling, undreamed lady
whose dark-throated murmuring is song. Picture
it: Just a couple of music lovers, all but
wasting in moonlight, with poetry damp and cooling
right up under our noses, soft lips, a mustache
—Ay, the possibilities of Spanish, the loving
tongue! Listen . . . "Adiós, adiós, mi corazón."

Lester Leaps In

Nobody but Lester let Lester leap
into a spotlight that got too hot
for him to handle, much less keep
under control like thirst in a drought.

He had his sensitive side, he had
his hat, that glamorous porkpie whose
sweatband soaked up all that bad
leftover energy.

           How did he choose
those winning titles he'd lay on favorites
—Sweets Edison, Sir Charles, Lady Day?
Oooo and his sound! Once you savor its
flaming smooth aftertaste, what do you say?

Here lived a man so hard and softspoken
he had to be cool enough to hold his horn
at angles as sharp as he was heartbroken
in order to blow what it's like being born.

The Blues Don't Change

"Now I'll tell you about the
Blues. All Negroes like Blues.
Why? Because they was born with
the Blues. And now everybody
have the Blues. Sometimes they
don't know what it is."
  —Leadbelly

And I was born with you, wasn't I, Blues?
Wombed with you, wounded, reared and forwarded
from address to address, stamped, stomped
and returned to sender by nobody else but you,
Blue Rider, writing me off every chance you
got, you mean old grudgeful-hearted, table-
turning demon, you, you sexy soul-sucking gem.

Blue diamond in the rough, you *are* forever.
You can't be outfoxed don't care how they cut
and smuggle and shine you on, you're like a
shadow, too dumb and stubborn and necessary
to let them turn you into what you ain't
with color or theory or powder or paint.

That's how you can stay in style without sticking
and not getting stuck. You know how to sting
where I can't scratch, and you move from frying
pan to skillet the same way you move people
to go to wiggling their bodies, juggling their
limbs, loosening that goose, upping their voices,
opening their pores, rolling their hips and lips.

They can shake their boodies but they can't shake *you.*

131